GOD
IN MY
GRIEF

The Music of Grace
When Loss Lives On

Thomas J. Davis

Judson Press
Valley Forge

Bible quotations in this volume are from the Revised Standard Version of the Bible, copyright © 1946, 1952, 1971, by the Division of Christian Education of the National Council of the Churches of Christ in the U.S.A. Used by permission.

Library of Congress Cataloging-in-Publication Data

Davis, Thomas J. (Thomas Jeffery); 1958-
    God in my grief : the music of grace when loss lives on / Thomas J.
Davis.
        p.   cm.
    Includes bibliographical references.
    ISBN 0-8170-1291-5 (pbk. : alk. paper)
    1. Bereavement – Religious aspects – Christianity. 2. Widows – Religious life.
    3. Davis, Thomas J. (Thomas Jeffery), 1958- . I. Title.
    BV4908.D33   1998
    248.8′66 – dc21   98-36320

Printed in the U.S.A.

06   05   04   03   02   01   00   99   98

5   4   3   2   1

CONTENTS

PREFACE

MY WIFE, THE REVEREND MELANIE ANN LANE, died in 1993 of acute lymphoblastic leukemia after a nineteen-month struggle with the disease. There are many good books that detail the illness and death of a loved one and reflect on the relation of faith to the devastating grief one experiences when watching a loved one die. It has been my experience, however, that the nature of grief changes somewhat over time. What I experienced during Melanie's illness and death, and the grief of the first year that followed, carried a "newness." Though the grief was real and painful, it was something I had not experienced before. Therefore, there was a period of adjustment during which I tried on the role of the grieving person, and it took some time to adjust to that role. It was like listening to a song I didn't know, and there was a sense of exploration — plumbing the depths, gauging the boundaries — that, for me, softened the harshness of death's song. Or, maybe the newness didn't soften the harshness; perhaps I was simply too much in shock to hear anything that first year.

There is a sense of permanency that sets in after the first year that calls a different tune for grief. This book explores what is, for me, the more permanent side of grief and the ways Christian faith relates to that grief.

There are a variety of ways in which people explore the world. Psychologists who study how people learn and relate to the world point out that most people have, among their five senses, a "primary" sense through which they filter, understand, and learn from their experiences. I know for myself that I am very aurally oriented: I pick up on things primarily through my sense of hearing, and the strongest associations I make between the world out there and my inner self is through sound. This is particularly so with music: I connect important events in my life, strong feelings, and relationships through bits of song and music. This book is an attempt to give shape to the notes of grief that play through my mind.

I am convinced that the sound of my grief is important, not just for me but for others. Grief is so incredibly isolating. It is hard to communicate loss in sounds that resonate with other people. I find it hard to sit down and share my feelings with others, which just contributes to my sense of isolation. In fact, I think it is difficult even to hear one's own grief without being deafened. There are those I know who have suffered a loss of a spouse who cannot give voice to that which most fills their days. This book is a song sung in the key of grief. May the notes be intelligible for those who have trouble singing their own song, and may they be audible to those who want to hear another's grief but cannot pick up on the broken melody played out in silence. This book is written in the knowledge that a song shared is a strong bond between hearts.

A book is always, I think, a collaborative effort, whether it be with those closest to you now or those who have influenced your thought through their writings. In the latter category, six people have been constant companions and appear frequently as conversation partners in these pages. My theology has been shaped by St. Augustine, Martin Luther, and John Calvin; my imagination has been stirred by George MacDonald, C. S. Lewis, and Frederick Buechner.

Of those closest to me, there are many I should thank for their collaboration. There is one I must thank, for, more than any other person, she has heard my song. For listening to me, not only with ears but also with the heart of friendship, I thank Terry.

INTRODUCTION

He rises and begins to sound,
  He drops the silver chain of sound,
Of many links without a break,
  In chirrup, whistle, slur and shake...
At sight of sun, her music's worth
  As up he wings the spiral stair,
A song of light, and pierces air...
  To reach the shining tops of day
And drink in everything discerned
  An ecstasy to music turned...
For singing till his heaven fills,
  'Tis love of earth that he instills,
Our valley is his golden cup
  And he the wine which overflows
To lift us with him as he goes...

Till lost on his aerial rings
  In light, and then the fancy sings.

— GEORGE MEREDITH (1828–1909)
"The Lark Ascending"[1]

A RAY OF SUNSHINE peeks over the hills and reveals a valley of dazzling beauty. Springtime freshness radiates from the budding trees, and early flowers push their heads through dirt to face the sun and sing its glory. This hill-ringed valley cradles a creek that winds its way through the terrain, running with a gladness that sounds like laughter. Gentle dawn outlines an apple tree in bloom, and on one of its branches sits a lark. Then, as that first beam of sunlight strikes and dawn becomes day, the bird takes off

toward the hill from which the sun has opened its sleepy morning eye.

All is smooth sailing until the morning breeze kicks up. At first, it pushes the lark downward, toward the earth. Then, the flying song is pushed off course slightly as the wind gusts. Finally, the lark catches the air that beats against him, and he uses the current to his own advantage, climbing higher into the sky. The lark disappears over the hill just as the sun rises in full power to rule the day, and he is enveloped in pure light.

This is the physical image that always comes to mind as I listen to Ralph Vaughn Williams's "The Lark Ascending," an orchestral piece Williams wrote when inspired by George Meredith's poem. The music that strikes me most powerfully paints pictures on the canvas of my mind's eye, and this music by Williams splashes more beautiful colors inside my head than any other.

What's more, "The Lark Ascending" is also intimately tied to my idea of Christian faith. I bring the music up here as an introduction to this work because, I think, I must set the right tone if I am to succeed in communicating my feelings.

The music of "The Lark Ascending" is, in many ways, the aural presentation of the faith that resides within my heart. This is not to say that Williams wrote the piece as an expression of faith — he did not. Rather, the structure of the song, its melody, its contrasts, and its expressions provide a form by which I interpret my faith. The music represents a longing to go skyward, to fly into the light of day. The mood is tentative, fragile at times. There are moments where the wings may not beat with certainty, yet there is the final triumph, when "lost on his aerial rings, In light," the lark ascends. So too, I believe, Christian souls ascend to God and bask in the eternal light. That is my faith.

I believe it is important to underline this music, this image, this feeling, this thought, because so much of this book may come across as despairing and desperate. I want it to be absolutely clear that my pain, bereavement, and grief — all that seems so terribly oppressive to me — is set within the context of this faith. While I, as a grieving person, feel hopeless much of the time, the deepest part of me does not think hopelessness is the final state God has in store for any of God's children. Still, this exploration of grief, with its attendant, sometimes chilling, examination of hopelessness, must be understood within the framework of a God who dies on a cross, helpless and, probably, hopeless-looking before the world — only to show forth the joy of life in glorious resurrection, a resurrection that is a token and a seal of all Christian hope. But before there is resurrection, there is death, and there is the tomb. I think of my grief at times as a tomb, but the tomb is a step toward new life.

Except perhaps in my darkest moments (or better, *even* in the depths of my darkest moments), there is an ear turned aside, waiting for the sound that is the balm of all desperate souls, the rumbling of rock when the stone rolls away and God calls forth life. My support in times of grief is not my ability to shake off hopelessness, for I cannot. My support is a faith in God who stirs the tomb of hopelessness. I look to that God for hope, not to myself or my own ability to fabricate false hope in a continuously heartrending situation. At least, in my better moments that's what I do. Martin Luther was right: "Did we in our own strength confide, our striving would be losing; were not the right man on our side, the man of God's own choosing.... The spirit and the gifts are ours through him who with us sideth."[2]

My grief is real. I hope you hear its notes. But my faith is also real, and I hope you hear, through my words and even in my despair, the music of God's grace. The wrestling of faith and despair, the interweaving dance of hopelessness and grace, is the lot of the Christian on earth. Facing and giving voice to the struggle is not a lack of faith but its proclamation.

Notes

1. George Meredith, *The Works of George Meredith*, vol. 25: *Poems II* (1912; repr., New York: Russell and Russell, 1968), 67–70.

2. Martin Luther, "A Mighty Fortress Is Our God," 1529.

Chapter One

THE SEASON OF GRIEF

MY WARM JACKET

My grief is a warm jacket;
I slip it on; it fits so snug.
I step outside and take a walk
  in the fall air of life.

It's nippy, but my jacket's a comfort
  When the air is too sharp;
    When the wind bites,
  My memories are a muffler.

Wrapped up I can walk along,
  Friends I see — I wave Hi!
Able to make it through the trails
  of daily existence.

I see the cold creep up the trees,
  The chill hand of winter's not far off.
The trees know the dread of that fall air
  That breathes death — for a season.

I go home, in the safety of solitude
I can slip my jacket off, put up my muffler,
  To sit in loneliness, by myself, inside —
    No jacket to ward off the cold.

Maybe one day it'll be summer again,
And I can walk the woods without my jacket,
  Grief cast aside, the warm sun shining —
    One day, if ever the season changes.

—TJD

Abraham knew the nethermost caverns of grief if any man has ever known them. Maybe it takes a god to know them.

— FREDERICK BUECHNER, *Son of Laughter*[1]

 I LIVE IN THE SEASON OF GRIEF. I wish it were like the other seasons of the year: a brief three months, maybe four, and then a distinct change rides the air. Each season of the year has its precursor. The burst of beautiful colors in the woods and the heavy, white breath blown out signals fall. The first snowflake that gently kisses earth will soon be a blanket that covers the sleeping ground during winter. The first bloom of the jonquil shouts with its yellow head that spring is coming. The first really hot day, when your shirt is good and drenched with sweat, proclaims the coming of summer.

I wish there was as clear a precursor to the change of emotional seasons, but there's not. I live in the season of grief, and I yearn for signs that the season is about to come to a close, give way to a sunnier, warmer season. What I long for is a happier season, when laughter fills the air, when the soul is carefree in its enjoyment of the goodness of God that surrounds it.

Yet this is only part of the way I feel. Mixed emotions rage within me. I fear that I will always be in the season of grief, where the landscape is unchanging, where the winds of pain and the rain of sorrow continually erode who I am. I want to move on with my life, change the seasons of my life; that's part of me. But another part of me is afraid to move on. My grief is a warm jacket, and in some ways it is the only comfort I have against reality. I want both to move out of grief and stay in my grief forever.

I want to move out of my grief because, emotionally, it is so debilitating. I feel like half a person while I grieve. I really think that I have pulled away from people, afraid that attachment will bring new sorrows. I am a ghost at times around people. They are real and I am not. When I meet new people, my hand goes out to meet theirs, but my spirit sits in a corner in my mind, unwilling fully to extend myself to new people. Will they be alive in a year, I wonder? My heart is stunted; I am a scrub tree on the inside. I am not whole while in grief; at least that's how I feel. I know it is a process I must move through, but it scares me.

My fear comes out in many ways, but mostly in ways that relate to loss. Since Melanie died, I am afraid that I will get sick or that the children will get sick. Sickness scares me. I feel out of control of my body and of my children's bodies. I want to make them safe, but I know that the last person I wanted to make safe died with me beside her. I was not able to protect or help her. Days are fragile when each child's cough brings out visions of that child's funeral, when each unexplained ache in my body forces my mind to jump to the conclusion that I have the type of bone pain symptomatic of Melanie's leukemia.

These underlying fears — fear of relationships, fear of my body, other fears I'll talk about later, like the fear of losing my mind — all seem related to my grief. At times I think I should try to flee and move to another state, move back to my old hometown. Perhaps I can outrun the grief, keep it behind me, so I don't have to face it.

Another odd fear is that of losing my grief. Though I want, in some ways, to be rid of the burden of grief, in another way it has become my only comfort, for it identifies who I am: I am a grieving person. In this sense, my grief is a warm jacket, but I don't want the seasons to change. I want to stay in the season of grief so I can hang on to the jacket of feelings I have become accustomed to, feelings of loss, bereavement, sadness, numbness.

I have two basic fears: that I will lose Melanie and that I will lose myself. I'm afraid that if I let go of my grief I will be letting go of Melanie, that my last link to her will be severed, that the only way she remains on this earth for me is through my grief. Sometimes her voice seems a bit fuzzy in my mind. Other times, I can't quite recall an anniversary dinner, what we talked about, how we felt. But I do know intimately the loss that knocked the breath out of me as I watched her die. That feeling is there, and it is strong. It is the last link on the chain that connects me to her. I can't let her go.

Also, because my grief defines me now, I'm afraid that if I take the jacket off, there will be nothing there, that I have become nothing but a grieving person. My grief is my ego, my center of activity, a set of expectations and a social role that I would be lost without — indeed, without it, I would be nothing. There is no "me" anymore, only a "grieving me."

These two feelings are at war inside me. Part of me wants to peel off my jacket of grief and run free from it, like a child on the first really warm day of spring who throws off the jacket his mom made him wear to school so he can run free with his friends. The other part of me wants to cling to my jacket as if the mere touch of fresh air would undo me and blow my flesh away, so I'd be no more real than a collection of bones clattering to the floor. My grief is a warm jacket, but how long will it be before it becomes a straitjacket? This situation is so well summed up by John Updike in his book *Rabbit Is Rich:* "Life. Too much of it, and not enough. The fear that it will end some day, and the fear that tomorrow will be the same as yesterday."[2] That description constitutes my insides: the fear that my grief will end one day — thus bringing an end to Melanie and maybe an end to me — constantly battling the fear that the same dull, pounding emptiness of grief, day in and day out, will simply be my lot for the rest of my life.

Some days I think that Melanie and I were so connected that I cannot exist as a "me" without her, that I am, even now, no more than what she was.

NIGHT TREMBLES

A late night talk host is my lover
She reaches me through cable tv
And thanks to her I'm not left to discover
that, alone, there is no me.

Grief wraps around me, an ice cold blanket
Freezing my soul, stuck to itself
Keeps me from wandering, looking for myself.
So I don't have to find that I am only
what she was.

I gaze at the stars, but there is no heaven
Stuck here on earth, in hell, alone.
Longing for death, a sweet caress,
Taking me from what I am
to that which I was.

The trembles, the shakes, come at night
The thrashings of a feverish soul
Longer, stronger than my beloved's death throes
With no antidote, no cure, except she who was
She who was, she who was.

To find my way alone in the world. That seems my task now. Yet I am not alone, and I thank God for that. I have my children, my family, my friends. Still, even though I surround myself with people, I am alone and lonely. There is always that nagging feeling that without "she who was" I cannot be otherwise than alone and lonely.

Where is God in my grief? I have asked that question many times. Where is God? It is an important question for me, because I cannot *not* believe in God. So where is God? To simply say that God doesn't exist is no answer for me. I have tried to figure out where God is, what the signs of God's presence could be, how to enshroud myself with that mystic union where God and I are joined. I have finally come up with a tentative answer, one that is both easy and hard, comforting and chilling, an affirmation and a negation. Quite simply, God — insofar as we can know God — is, among other places, in grief itself.

The story of the Crucifixion means many things. Since the meaning of the universe is there played out, that is as it should be. The meaning of the universe is to be seen in the face of Jesus on the cross, a face that invites people to look upon it, to bring questions to it, to lay bare our own selves before it. Since we are all fragile humans, each broken in his or her own way, what we see may depend on the state of our souls at the time. When I bring my broken self to the foot of the cross and look up at the broken Jesus, what I see in his face is grief, pure and simple.

I see both human and divine grief. The human face of Jesus is torn apart by a scream from the cross, one that tears apart my heart as well: "My God, my God, why hast thou forsaken me?" (Mark 15:34)[3] Jesus felt forsaken. His disciples had fled; the crowds now jeered instead of cheered; there were no angels to brighten the sky or sing of peace. In the midst of it all, did Jesus see God? For a while, at least, he did not.

Jesus was citing the first verse of Psalm 22. The words of that grief seem so much like mine that they bear repetition:

> My God, my God, why hast thou forsaken me?
>   Why art thou so far from helping me,
>   from the words of my groaning?
> O my God, I cry by day, but thou dost not answer;
>   and by night, but find no rest.
>   Yet thou art holy....
>   —Psalm 22:1–3

This is a cry of anguish and a cry of recognition: recognition that there is one who is holy, who sits in transcendence above the world yet also reaches down to the world; anguish because that one thing that is the proper and true desire of all hearts seems to have simply gone away. The anguish of Jesus, my anguish, the anguish of the world at times, is that we've been left alone. The question of the grieving person is not "Does God exist?" Rather, it is "My God, my God, why hast thou forsaken me?"

Reading Psalm 22 carefully for the first time after my grief had years to settle in, I was struck that in that ancient poetry the very words that describe my grief appear, not just in the cry of rejection but also in the simple description of the heart. The psalmist says, "My heart is like wax, it is melted within my breast" (Psalm 22:14). That is exactly how my grief feels. It has made for me a heart of wax. And Jesus, I believe, shares it. While looking to the sky, his heart also must have been waxen, melted in his breast, grief stricken by the absence of one whose presence he preached.

But the face of Jesus, at least as I understand it, is not just the human face looking up at God's desertion; it is also a divine face, the face of God, looking out at desertion. The face of Jesus on the cross is the face of God's grief. A grieving person feels, above all else, even when all other feeling is gone, loss. How can I say God grieves in the face of Jesus? Because God looking out from the cross must have felt loss.

What did God see from the cross? God saw creation at war, dear children killing each other. God saw cruelty, a world gone awry, evil rewarded and good punished. Most of all, I think God saw the face of a mother lifted up to her son, a good son, a righteous son, who was in his death throes, executed by means of a horrible and humiliating instrument. God saw the horror of a mother's grief brought on by a world God had made. From the cross, God mourned the loss of God's good creation.

Perhaps the blame for such a situation belongs to God. Many claim that. But what I think is that God grieved on the cross because God saw through human eyes the mystery of freedom, which had been created as the highest good, being turned into the vulgarity of bondage to all that is base, evil, and ugly. On the cross, God had the opportunity, through the face of Jesus, to show God's grief to the world and cry out about God's own forsakenness — to cry out about a world that had forsaken its Creator.

The human face of Jesus and the divine face of Jesus both

looked out in forsakenness, loss, and grief. Both looked for a beloved who did not look back, as I look for my beloved who does not look back. And the explanation I come up with is all those things mentioned above — easy and hard, comforting and chilling, an affirmation and a negation — because life is all those things.

For better or worse, in the final analysis, the basis of grief is love. If I did not love Melanie, I would not grieve for her. If Jesus did not love God, he would not have grieved their separation. If God did not love us, God would not grieve our loss and separation. "For God so loved the world that he gave his only Son" (John 3:16). The playing out of that statement in the realm of human existence is the story of love mixed with grief — grief over a lost world, grief over a lost son, grief over a lost father. God was willing to undergo grief in order to overcome it. The way to the attainment of that victory of love was not through skirting grief but through incarnating into it. Where is my God while I grieve? Not above or beyond it, with a heavenly rope ladder slung downward so that I can climb out of my grief. That is what I wish, but it is not so. If I have the courage to look into the face of grief, God is *in* my grief. Frederick Buechner has said so aptly that there is something more terrifying than the face of death — the face of love.[4] Sometimes I blink. Sometimes I run scared. But in those rare moments when I can screw up my courage enough to look, I can look into the grieving face of God/Jesus on the cross and see the face of love.

There's an Irish poem about love and grief, a line of which runs, "And she said let grief be a falling leaf at the dawning of the day."[5] You can imagine the cool autumn air, frost sparkling on the ground, when a slight breeze picks up and gently tugs the last leaf of fall from the tree and carries it down to the ground. The wind is the Spirit of God. It carries me in my grief, and it will finally carry my grief away, one day in that land where there will be no more tears. But until I am carried away as a leaf on the wind of God's Spirit,

I endure the season of grief, because God enters into that season and walks with me as a fellow griever. That is the gospel.

Notes

1. Frederick Buechner, *Son of Laughter: A Novel* (San Francisco: HarperSanFrancisco, 1994), 171.
2. John Updike, *Rabbit Is Rich* (New York: Random House, 1981), 331.
3. See also Matthew 27:46.
4. Frederick Buechner, *The Magnificent Defeat* (San Francisco: HarperSanFrancisco, 1966), 18.
5. Patrick Kavanagh, "Raglan Road," in *Collected Poems* (New York: Devin-Adair, 1964), 186.

Chapter Two

A CRY IN THE DARK

Like a size-twelve workboot kicked into my gut I felt it, and I clutched my stomach, unable to breathe. The light turned green and cars started honking; a few drove around me; someone leaned out of a truck window and shouted, "Hey, you! Are you okay?" I couldn't speak. I couldn't move. All I could think as I stood there holding myself was, "I want my mother. I want my mother. I want my mother, now."

— HOPE EDELMAN, *Motherless Daughters*[1]

And I heard a loud voice from the throne saying, "Behold, the dwelling of God is with men. He will dwell with them, and they shall be his people, and God himself will be with them; he will wipe away every tear from their eyes, and death shall be no more, neither shall there be mourning nor crying nor pain any more, for the former things have passed away."

— Revelation 21:3–4

 A PROFESSOR OF MINE IN SEMINARY, talking about suffering for the gospel, spoke these words: "It's not how much you are willing to suffer for the gospel, but how much you are willing to let your children suffer." This professor came out of the Barthian tradition, which not only produced volumes of dogma but much real involvement in the suffering of those fighting against Nazi Germany. Though I do not now suffer for the sake of the gospel — at least not in the sense that he meant it — I do have to wrestle with the suffering of my children and how to relate faith in God to them in the midst of their suffering.

11

My children have been raised in the Christian faith. There has hardly been a Sunday when they've missed church. We pray, we talk about God and Jesus. Now my children are nine and twelve. The youngest hasn't quite gotten all her theological vocabulary down. One day she said she knew that God was near. *A nice sentiment*, I thought. "How do you know?" I asked.

"Because I can feel the sun, and everybody knows that Jesus is God's sun."

A nice sentiment, as I said, but it was also an occasion for learning about homonyms.

Yet no matter the depth of their theology, the depth of their experience and suffering is as deep as it needs to be for ones so young. They know enough to ask, "Why? Why did God let Mommy die?" I struggle with watching them suffer through those questions. I want to give them easy answers, comforting answers, but I have a problem pawning off answers on them that don't work for me. There are no easy answers to their questions, only more questions. My gut reaction is that they, just as I, must suffer through this loss, hoping they will meet God in their grief. That is much harder than simply trying to relieve their minds with pat answers. I try to be an instrument of God's grace in their lives rather than an obstacle, but I am usually at a loss as to how best to do that.

In many ways, their situation mirrors my own, only they don't have the experience and knowledge to filter their feelings. Though I grieve more consistently than they, I think, and perhaps deeper at times, by and large their grief may be more immediate, if less conscious. Because they don't have the words to organize, filter, tame, or explain their grief, it hits them more like a kick in the stomach than anything else.

It's very hard to get used to. You're in bed, fast asleep, hoping there will be no dreams to remind you of what you have lost. On the edge of consciousness, you hear a voice. All of a sudden, you're wide awake. The parental instinct to sit upright, heart beating hard at the screams of your children, is very basic. Adrenalin pumps. You're ready for a crisis, ready to act, ready to save, if you can. Then you hear the words buried in the screams: "Mommy! Mommy! Mommy! Where are you, Mommy? I want my Mommy!" You rush into the bedroom and scoop your child into your arms, heart racing, prepared for a crisis. You're ready to act. Your child awakens fully, looks around for Mommy, and sees you. You see the disappointment in her face, realizing there will be no saving on this night. This cry in the dark, against which I can do nothing, strikes like a dagger to my overreactive heart. I rock my child, sing to her, tell her she's all right, and lull her back to sleep. Then I go back to my room, heart still pounding from the adrenalin rush, and wish to God that Mommy had been there to comfort her daughter.

When we lie in our own darkness, the darkness of our lives, the darkness of the world that surrounds us, the darkness of our own hearts, don't we all cry out like that? "Mommy! God! Where are you? Where are you?" We all cry in the dark for the one we miss.

If called upon, I sometimes think I would be capable of doing deeds of violence to protect my children. At times, I think I would be capable of great acts of sacrifice for the protection of my children. Yet what blow can I strike or endure to protect them from their own fears that issue in a cry in the dark?

How can I protect them from their fears? They are there, even in children — fear and guilt. These feelings may be more direct for them than for me because there's no language or symbol to filter out the pain. Fear is expressed in their cries; guilt comes out in dreams.

Mave, my oldest, once called for Mommy while dreaming. As I spoke to her about her dream, I learned it was a nightmare full of guilt. She could relate the dream in vivid detail, for she had had the dream more than once.

Five men came after her and Mommy — bad men — and

kidnapped them. They were tied up and taken away. Then they were separated. Mave told about how scared she was, but she kept thinking, "I've got to get to Mommy." Finally the men guarding her left, and she was able to get away. The rest of the dream involved Mave going from building to building, frantically looking for Mommy. She finally found her at the end of the dream, dead. That's when the cries of "Mommy! Mommy!" would begin. I would go to her bedroom to hold her and to tell her it's all right, and while the fear subsided a bit — at least the immediate fear of the bad men from the dream — the guilt that lay therein did not.

Sometimes we adults forget what it is like to be a child and to recall the depth of feeling that a child can have. For example, adults wink at the idea of young love, "puppy love," the very name diminishing the thing itself. Yet I still think of the first person I ever loved this way, almost thirty years after she moved away.

I can try to protect Mave from bad men; I can try to build into her world a sense of security. But how do I protect her from her own mind and feelings? To me, it is a suffering child who, at a young age, must take on the guilt for her mother's death. The dream makes it obvious: She let Mommy down. She didn't protect Mommy. She didn't rescue Mommy. This comes down, quite simply, to the following: She's responsible for Mommy's death.

How do I guard her from those feelings? Can I? Should I? Or does she have to work through these feelings on her own? If so, what a terrible burden for a school-age child. Will she wrestle with these feelings for the rest of her life? Will she be standing in the middle of the road one day when she feels the size-twelve boot kick in the stomach, the result of years of guilt, fear, and helplessness? I pray not; I try to help so it will not be so. I want so badly to take on her suffering, but she is the one who must bear it. She loved Melanie deeply, and to love, one must be willing to risk all of these awful feelings if the loved one is taken away.

Taken away. That's an awfully hard concept for a child. If Mave's struggles to come to grips with Melanie's death have initially been to overcome — or at least neutralize — the many negative scary feelings she has, Gwynne, my youngest, first had to work through what it means to be dead.

One of these days, I am afraid that Gwynne may have to deal with a guilt particular to her actions as a very small child — because of the way she will feel, not because of the way I will make her feel. I made a two-hour videotape of Melanie, once we knew she was going to die. I wanted more. I meant to get more, but two hours is it. There are happy times: Christmas morning, some times at church. But very quickly the tape turns to the hospital room.

I can't remember why I had the tape on (I think Melanie wanted it on) but it was running when Melanie had to tell the children there was nothing else the doctors would be able to do. She was going to die, and she would die soon. Gwynne, bless her heart, started jumping up and down on the bed singing, "Mommy's going to die, Mommy's going to die." Then she started asking questions. "Will you die on the road?" I can only guess that most of the dead things Gwynne had seen had been dead animals on the road. I started to protest Gwynne's reaction, but Melanie said, "No. We all have to deal with this in our own way. If this is how Gwynne feels like acting, that's how she should act." Wise words. I hope Gwynne hears them when she is old enough to look at the tape and sees how she reacted as a three-year-old.

Gwynne, of course, did not know what it really meant to die. That is the lesson she has had to learn in the past five years. At first, she had fantasies of Mommy coming back. At one point, nearly a year and a half after Melanie's death, Gwynne had some questions about some of Melanie's clothes I had kept, a few very special things that I just couldn't bring myself to send away. After fingering them for a while, Gwynne asked, "Do you think it will be okay if I wear these when I'm bigger?" Sure, I said, why not? Then a look of concern came over her face. "If Mommy comes back, I'll share." I asked Gwynne what she meant. She knew Mommy was dead, she said, but just in case she came back alive, she didn't want Mommy to worry about not having clothes. Gwynne would share. Tears welled up in my eyes. *God bless this child*, I thought.

The finality eventually does set it. At another point in time, Gwynne asked what seemed to be an innocent question concerning the physics of Melanie's deterioration. "Has Mommy turned into bones yet?" she asked. I had explained to Gwynne what would happen to Melanie's body. I also talked to her about her spirit being with God and how, one day, she would have a new body to go with her spirit. I thought it was a question of information. As happens so often, I was mistaken.

"Has Mommy turned into bones yet?" An innocent-seeming question from a small child of four. She didn't appear to be upset or worried or grieving.

"No," I replied, "she hasn't. Not yet." I started to give more information than Gwynne had requested. I verged on talking, in what I thought was four-year-old language, about embalming, sealed and waterproofed caskets, and all that.

I was stopped by a sudden burst of tears as Gwynne pleaded, "Let's go dig her back up, then. Please! Please!" She wanted her mommy back, and if Mommy wasn't a pile of bones yet, Gwynne saw no reason why we couldn't have her back. Through much pain and suffering and agony, she knows now that Mommy cannot be dug back up and will not come back to claim her clothes. Mommy is dead. Perhaps it feels like a permanent kick in the stomach.

Sometimes such a feeling is too much for one so young to handle. Gwynne is now nine. She has adjusted well and enjoys being a third grader, yet she misses her mommy. Not with the same urgency or expectation, she asked one night at song time if there really wasn't a way to make a person come back to life. She knew the answer was "no" before she asked, but she wanted to be sure. During this big transition period in her life, no doubt she would like to have some help other than Dad's, but she's pretty sure she's not going to get it. Little children can sometimes hide their feelings for the benefit of adults. I knew Gwynne was missing Melanie. I didn't know how much until Parent Night when she was in second grade. There on the wall was a picture of Gwynne. She had been traced on a big sheet of paper. She then colored in all the parts, giving herself green eyes. The paper was folded so that it looked like Gwynne had on a jacket. When the jacket opened, there were pictures of the family and information about Gwynne. I thought the whole thing awfully darned cute. I like cute, especially with children this age. "My name is Gwynne," I was informed. "I have brown eyes. I have brown hair." The last bit of information broke my heart. "I am happy when I don't think of Mommy because then I don't cry." A child can only take so much of the pain of grieving, and then she must turn away.

Of course she can't, not really — and be a healthy little girl. She must face the empty place at the dinner table and come to grips with Melanie's absence and the way her absence always presents itself to us. Melanie is present now through her very absence. Her not being where she's supposed to be, in all the places a mom tries to be for her daughters and husband, is a constant, abiding presence with us. In the end, Gwynne can't help but to think of Melanie, and so she must go through her times of unhappiness.

Though I have for quite some time enlisted the aid of a professional counselor for the children, Gwynne and Mave both must face their loss. As much as I try, I cannot take away their hurt, pain, suffering, and grief. They must work through it themselves. I am left outside to watch as their insides are torn to shreds, only slowly to heal and join back together. To watch this happening, though, gives me greater insight into Job's wife. She was the one who railed at Job to curse God and die. Job refused. The insight? It may, in the final analysis, be easier to bear and understand and even defend one's own suffering in the face of God than it is to do that for your loved ones.

As much as I want to take away their tears, I cannot. I cannot bring their mother back to life, which is, right now, the only cure for their tears. The best I can do is be with them, support them, and try to understand the uniqueness of their grief. But I cannot take away their tears. The best I can do is to teach them about one who can. I can suffer with them, but I must leave it to God to redeem them, and that is the hardest lesson of all, I think, for a parent.

Jesus said, "Let the children come to me" (Matthew 19:14).[2] If I have the faith to let my children go and sit at the knee of Jesus, many wonderful things will result. But there is a risk. If Jesus' face is the face of God's grief, if God is with us by suffering along with us — not rescuing us from suffering — then I cannot expect to see my children's pain simply vanish. A step toward Christ, even for a child, is a step toward full humanity, with the capacity for love that makes grief so powerful. If I send my children to Jesus to learn of God's love (and they will) they will also learn the source of grief — a love that cannot let go.

In the final analysis, the children show us the way, for we are all God's children. In the face of all that grieves us, even as adults, we let out a cry in the dark, "God!" The best we can do for our children and ourselves is to let out that cry, so its sound may lead us from darkness to light.

Notes

1. Hope Edelman, *Motherless Daughters: The Legacy of Loss* (Reading, Mass.: Addison-Wesley, 1994), 4.

2. See also Mark 10:14 and Luke 18:16.

Chapter Three

WHO AM I?

And Jesus went on with his disciples, to the villages of Cae-
sarea Philippi; and on the way he asked his disciples, "Who
do men say that I am?" And they told him, "John the Baptist; and others say, Elijah; and others one of the prophets."
And he asked them, "But who do you say that I am?" Peter
answered him, "You are the Christ."   — Mark 8:27–29[1]

 "WHO AM I?" That's a pretty basic question
that everyone has to face at one time or an-
other. We think of teenagers trying to work
their way through the world, searching for an
identity, thinking that in thoughtlessly casting
off their parents' expectations and mindlessly
putting on the image of their peers they have found their
identity. We think perhaps of little children, who must for-
mulate their self-image in relationship to the world, once
they discover there is a world. Sometimes in middle age
people stop to evaluate who they are. In a less dramatic but
perhaps more important way, all of us seek to know who we
are as we muddle through the decisions, compromises, joys,
and sorrows that are part and parcel of daily existence.

"Who am I?" That is one of the two or three big religious questions, along with "Who is God?" and "What is
my purpose here?" John Calvin made it part of his theology,
following the many before him who made similar claims.
"Nearly all the wisdom we possess," he said, "that is to say,
true and sound wisdom, consists of two parts: the knowledge
of God and of ourselves."[2]

For the grieving person, "Who am I?" is a question that demands an answer. It is an unsettling, troubling, troublesome question. It involves how you think about yourself, how other people try to define you, and what your ultimate relationship is to God and Christ. It is a question that demands to be answered. If you aren't ready to deal with it, to think about it, then others will remind you about it.

"Who am I?" That is a hard question to answer, in some ways, because of the conflicting messages we get about what an *I* is. In America, land of rugged individualism and the lone hero, people sometimes get the impression that there is such a thing as an *I* without a community of some sort to recognize that *I*. Is there an essence to me, a "Tomness" that defines me? I think not. My individuality is not mine in isolation; it is how I reflect on the relationships that make me who I am. Speaking of my individualism, or who I am as a person, is less a process of seeking within me than it is a matter of reflecting on who I am in relationship to other people and to God. When I speak of knowing myself, what I mean is knowing about the way I am related to others.

This is part of the reason why being a grieving person is so hard in relationship to the question, "Who am I?" The primary human relationship by which I understand myself is with a person who is now dead. I used to tell a very few select friends about how I am haunted by Melanie's death. The image of her dying still — five years later — is the image that makes itself most known to me. What I fight against, rather constantly, is that image defining not only her existence but also mine.

This image *is* unfair. Melanie was so much more than her death. She was a grace-filled child of God whose presence was a joy to all who knew her. My life is so different and so much better, infinitely better, for having had her as my wife. Why aren't all the good things she brought me more memorable than her death? Why am I so quick to remember the bad, while the good mostly floats at the perimeter of my mind, making occasional forays into my consciousness, but mostly hiding in the recesses? It is difficult for me to wrench the meaning of her life away from the ugliness of her death. I do her a disservice to let her death so dominate my mind. Yet it does.

Because my image of her is so death-filled at times, my image of myself also suffers. I fight, but I always feel I am losing. Melanie's death defines me, no matter how hard I try to write a new meaning to my life. Melanie's death draws me to death. Since she was so much a part of me, now I want to be a part of her in any way I can. There are serious implications for this feeling, but for now let's take smaller steps and look at some of the ways her death defines me.

If the word *salvation* means, among other things, "to make whole," then oftentimes I perceive myself as unsaved. Melanie's death sometimes defines me as a broken person, as incomplete. People sometimes call the wife the "better half." Though said jokingly, for the person who has lost a wife, this feeling of being broken in half is very strong. This state of being is reinforced constantly by myself, my children, and others around me.

It has been so hard for me to make major decisions since Melanie's death. I do not trust my own judgment. We made all our big decisions together. Through lively banter, discussion, jokes, an occasional hard feeling, heartful exploration, and prayerful consideration, we would come to a resolution about things. Because of the process of decision making we went through together, there was always a sense of making our major decisions together. School decisions, career choices, child-rearing philosophy, how to live in and respond to the world around us were all made easier by knowing that I walked in freedom and responsibility with a companion who walked with me and shared the consequences of joy and sorrow, hope and despair, fulfillment and disillusionment. The bond of love connected our hearts and doubled our courage and commitment, resolve and resilience. Once we made decisions, we tended to walk boldly, "heel to heel and toe to toe,"[3] in joyful recognition that, in many things, God frees us to walk where we would.

How hard the baby steps come now. After being a sprinter, I crawl now. Uncertain, afraid of the wrong choices I bear alone, I make tentative decisions. I constantly second-guess myself in a way I never did before. While married, did Melanie and I want to pick up and move from Tennessee to Chicago to chase a dream? Yes, and we went laughing and singing in the U-Haul truck to an apartment we had never seen and set up house in an environment unlike anything either of us had ever known. Would we go bust? Maybe. If we did, it would be arm in arm. We ran into life headlong.

After her death, the running seems to have stopped. Am I broken without her? Perhaps not entirely, at times. But almost always, I have this feeling that at least my legs of faith in myself have been broken. Every decision is meticulously weighed, measured, thought about, dreamed about, and second-guessed. If before we ran in the wonderful lightness of being, now I slog through the mud, weighed down by a self I don't fully recognize or trust. That is the problem: Who am I? I have to know that before either recognition or trust can begin to work.

The specter of Melanie's death defines me in other ways. If salvation means wholeness, it also means wellness. Here again, there is a redefinition of the self that grief imposes. I no longer look at "being well" and "being sick" in the same way. Before Melanie's illness and death, I always saw myself as a healthy person. In so much of life now, I feel like a sick person. I am consumed by images of death and dying, illness and sickness. I no longer see the health that is in me; I see, instead, the illness that lurks, waiting to capture me as it did Melanie.

This may sound like paranoia; it probably is paranoia. At times bereavement has the ability to make life completely untrustworthy and that is, more than anything, a breach of faith. Faith is trust and assurance that God is with you. Though faith involves knowing and believing, it cannot be reduced to that. Existentially, faith is something you lean back into, something that holds you, holds you up. It is a letting go of your own ability and leaning back into the ability of another, one whose arms hold and rock like a hammock. Faith means to lay back and trust — trust that the hammock ropes will hold, trust that the thing won't tip over, trust that the limbs that bear the weight are capable of bearing the weight.

In my bereavement and grief, life is more like a hammock that is full of holes, unsteady, with frayed twine attached either to rotten limbs or ones too tender to bear the full brunt of my weight. I do not trust it to hold me; I do not trust God to hold me. Not trusting God, I often do not trust my body. I expect it to be betrayed in the same way that Melanie's was.

For the first year or so after Melanie's death, I would occasionally see a few red spots on my legs, arms, or chest. "My God, I've got leukemia, just like Melanie," would be my first reaction. Little red dots on the skin are often a sign that platelet counts are low, and little spots of bleeding appear near the skin's surface. Did I have a cold or bronchitis? "Oh, My God, it's pneumonia. I'll die with a chest full of fluid, just like Melanie did," I'd think. Every ache, every little pain, became prophetic for me, prophesying an early death that would leave my children orphans. The first two years after Melanie's death, I probably visited the doctor's office more than in the entire rest of my life. I never went to the doctor before; now it was constant.

Looking back on this experience, two items jump to mind to explain this obsession with doctors and health. The first is that the world of medicine had been, for a very intense period over many months, very much a part of my life. It was one of the routines that made up my normal schedule. Breaking away from that schedule was difficult. That isolation from the world in which Melanie and I had lived such intense moments couldn't be left cold turkey. I visited the doctor's office because it was familiar and, in an odd way, comforting. The doctor's job was, above all else, to take care of me.

More than that, I think that my attitude toward my physical health simply served to mask a much more painful reality: the sickness of my soul. I was so broken inside. The nets of spiritual life — that hammock of faith — seemed so fragile that I was afraid of slipping through. All bodies die. In this regard, my worst dreams will eventually come true. The aches and pains we carry do prophesy a time when our bodies will quit on us, betray us, turn on us like a mad dog turns on its owner. What makes such knowledge bearable is knowing that our bodies are not the sum total of everything we are. We are also spiritual beings who, in cooperation with a body, trek through life until God makes the partnership between body and soul something more. The key to the success of that partnership between spirit and body is for the spirit to lend its strength to the body, nurture the body, and assure it that, though bodies die, our relationship with God does not. The meaning of our lives is not contingent on our bodies gliding through life unscathed but on a body scarred by nails and a voice that cries, "Come to me."[4] That is a spiritual understanding; that is the trust at the heart of faith. It is the thing that is so hard for the bereaved and grieving person to believe.

Perhaps the oddest craving, though it sounds contradictory, is for the very thing of which I am so afraid. If the notion of sin is related to brokenness, then I am sinful, not just because I anticipate brokenness rather than wholeness, but in the way I invite it, worry after it, embrace it. At times I want the marks of my inner brokenness to be displayed on my body, so I can feel a certain wholeness of despair, outer matching inner. Perhaps it is not so odd. I remember reading in James Michener's *Hawaii* about the native practice of maiming oneself after a spouse has died. In this particular scene, despite the work of Christian missionaries to discourage the practice, the husband of a tribal queen plucks out his eye.[5] At the time I read the book, I found the notion repulsive and illogical. Now, to the core of my being, I understand the impulse. It was a cry for continuity between inner and outer, body and soul.

A few times when I was ill, I consciously decided not to go to the doctor so that I could bear the sign of inner distress and disease on my flesh. I craved sickness and let myself remain sick when, in fact, I knew a trip to the doctor would soon make things right. But being sick seemed right. Not only did it become a type of physical reflection, a bodily mirror for the state of my soul, but it also joined me a little to Melanie. I wanted to feel sick so that I could share an experience with her. I wanted my feelings to be like her feelings; I wanted discomfort so I could share in hers. I'd lie in fever, thinking of the times her temperature would shoot up.

The saddest thing of all is that, by doing this, I stood for everything Melanie stood against. Trying to join her this way, a barrier separated us. She would not have approved. Everything in her being strove after a genuine existence, a true life. My attempts to be like her this way represented mockery, not tribute. The illness I fear and the illness I embrace are not contradictory, after all. They are both a fleeing from life, a loss of trust, and a sign that I am, in fact, in danger of losing myself. Who am I? At times like these, I look in the mirror and simply don't recognize the figure who looks back.

At the beginning of this chapter, I spoke of how the problem of identity is not simply a matter of how the grieving person views himself or herself but how others react. Our identity — my identity — is social. Going back to the story of Jesus' identity, Jesus asks his disciples, "Who do you say that I am?" For me, and I imagine for all who have lost a spouse, it seems that my very presence invokes the question, and people's responses often unwittingly label me as somehow less than I was with Melanie.

Though it may seem a small matter, one of the things that hurts me most, because it constantly calls attention to my being incomplete, is going to a restaurant. I've grown tired of counting the times I've stood with my children, waiting for a hostess to seat us, only to be ignored. When the hostess comes, she invariably looks around and asks, "Only three?" To this day, it rends my heart to have to say, "Yes, just the three of us."

This hurts because it comes so close to the way I feel at times — that we are not a complete family and that I am not a complete person. "Only three" implies that there should be four. They see a husband and children and look around for a wife, but she is not there to be seen. And so we go to a booth for four (there are no booths built for three), and the empty space is a palpable reminder that Melanie is missing. Maybe that is why, when we are in restaurants, my children so often draw pictures of our family, angel Melanie flying in heaven and looking down on the three of us. The empty space reminds them that someone is missing, and it not only makes us incomplete as individuals, but it also makes for a broken family. At least, that's how we feel at times.

The fundamental question for a person of faith, of course, is "How does God fit into this picture?" If I were like Mave or Gwynne, drawing pictures of our family with the three of us on earth and Melanie up above, where would I draw God, and how? I often tell the children that Melanie is with God. Melanie is absent from us. Does that mean God is, too?

When I think this way, I have to stop myself. I am caught up in the American cult of happiness as much as the next person. Since at least the beginning of the nineteenth century — in both formal theology and the more eclectic religious thoughts of lay people in American Christianity — personal happiness has replaced the glory of God as the goal toward which Christians strive. We no longer judge ourselves in light of glorifying God; we judge God by how happy we are. For the most part these days, God's goodness is interpreted according to our happiness, for surely a loving God wants us to be happy. Or, as I heard one fellow say, "Hey, maybe God does want us to have a Mercedes Benz." The irony of Janis Joplin's lyrics are all but lost for too many today.

The problem and its answer are simple. God is not found only in happiness, though I think God is in joy. Rather, God is found in moments of crisis. In fact, I think God is to be found in the throes of life's brokenness, which may, more than anywhere else, define our common humanity. When trying to understand where God is, the symbol I come back to is the sacrament of Communion. The image and the words of Communion serve as a strong mead that invigorates my soul. In the Eucharist I am brought face to face with God, and it is always an eye-opening experience.

The Eucharist graphically presents the very thing I try so hard to avoid — brokenness. When I am caught up in the cult of happiness, blaming God for not waving a magic wand and making me beam with self-pleasure, the Eucharist makes me confront myself and my images of what real life should be like. In the Eucharist, I am presented with a man who is a man but also God with us, who stands before people with the very symbols of life-sustaining sustenance, bread and wine, and proclaims through and with these life-drenched symbols, "This is my body which is given for you" (Luke 22:19). Jesus tells us that life, real life, true life, a life-breathing divinity, is tied, while on this earth, with brokenness — broken bread and a broken body.

Where is God? Not above the brokenness but *within* it. If I am to understand the current of divinity that energizes existence, I must face the broken man Jesus. John Calvin once said that God became human in Jesus so that God would not be "hidden and far off."[6] The Eucharist reminds me that I've been looking too far off for God, for I've been looking beyond pain and brokenness. God is not far off, and if I want to see God, I have to look within myself at the brokenness and realize that God is there. Here is the revelation of the Eucharist: God, God's forgiveness, God's power, and God's ability to heal is tied intimately, unswervingly, and completely with brokenness. This is my body, broken for you.

Here is power: to look at the very point of weakness and find strength; to look at brokenness and see wholeness; to look at the most desperate plight of humanity, a man broken on a cross, and find divinity.[7] That is the power of the Eucharist. The Eucharist is, indeed, as the ancients referred to it, the medicine of immortality[8] if we have the courage to swallow what seems to be the most bitter pill.

Now some of Paul's sayings make sense. His injunction in Romans 13:14 to "put on the Lord Jesus Christ" is about goodness, but it is also about living through the tragedies of life exemplified by the tragedy of the cross. Communion with Christ, which the Eucharist displays for us, is lived out as we put on Christ, and to put on Christ is to delve into the depths of life, to explore abundant life, and come to the heart of human existence, where there is wedded joy and brokenness. Christ is our joy, for he not only heals our brokenness, he takes it on and shares it with us.

Martin Luther liked to speak of the Christian's life in this world as being a dual existence. We are, he stated, both just and sinful at the same time.[9] If we take these words to be fairly translated as whole and broken, and I think we can, then we start to grasp what Luther was saying. By putting on Christ, we do not flee brokenness; it is a part of life in this world. But by putting on Christ we are given a foretaste of wholeness, because in Christ we see how the broken was made whole, not by running from a broken world, broken relationships, and a broken self, but by entering into the brokenness. By throwing ourselves into the brokenness, we enter the fire forged by God's goodness, wherein we can be reformed in God's likeness and image.

C. S. Lewis, speaking through one of his fictional characters, once asked, "How can they [the gods] meet us face to face till we have faces?"[10] The face of our humanity, collectively and individually, is forged by life in all its uncertainty and problems. Who we are is an ongoing process of relating to life. Having to live through things like the death of a loved one, which is so horrible, may be the only thing that can really convey to us the importance of the relationship of love, which is, in the end, what God would have define us all. If we would be able to look at God face to face, as Paul says in 1 Corinthians 13:12, maybe Lewis's instinct is right. To see God's face, we must first have our own, a face capable of seeing divine love and grace and mercy. If the face of God is in part scarred by grief because it is scarred by love, then the only way we can literally face God is to wear God's face, the face Christ puts on us.

In Genesis 32:22–30, there's that odd story about Jacob wrestling with God all night. Finally, God touches Jacob in such as way as to break him. Yet Jacob in his brokenness hangs on to God, asking for blessing. Jacob's name is changed to Israel, literally "one who strives with God" (cf. Genesis 32:28). Who we are, who I am, comes about as I understand, little by little, that the one who breaks me is also the one who blesses me. We all strive with God so that God will bless us. And how did God bless Jacob? By naming him.

Jesus strove with God in the Garden of Gethsemane. Sweat like great drops of blood flowed down his face. In Mark 14:36, I read "Remove this cup from me" as "Don't break me!" Yet Jesus was broken. And who is he? Well, how did the centurion, the one who stood at the foot of the cross and viewed the broken Jesus, name him? "Truly this man was the Son of God" (Mark 15:39).[11] What is proclaimed about me in church liturgy within my community? How am I named in the baptismal liturgy? As a child of God.[12] If I am to grow up in the household of God, growing in semblance to the family that claims me, then my face must also take on the characteristics of God's face, of Jesus' face. The God who breaks me blesses me with my name and my identity, for the breaking is not punishment but an invitation to see the cost of love. When I call out Melanie's name in love, it is an echo of God's call to me, and the depth of my feelings for her is but the smallest accommodation that God provides for insight into God's nature and disposition toward us. As I name God, I name love, which names Melanie and me. Jesus knows who I am because he loves me, and in that statement is mixed joy and sorrow, brokenness and wholeness, death and resurrection. In that statement is wonder, as Thomas à Kempis knew:

> Oh Love, how deep, how broad, how high,
> How passing thought and fantasy,
> That God, the Son of God, should take
> Our mortal form for mortals' sake.[13]

In times of faith, that affirmation is an affirmation of who I am in relation to God. When I hear the music of that love which passes all fantasy, I can, even in the face of Melanie's death and maybe even through the brokenness it represents, hear the melody of my life. But it is not always so.

Notes

1. See also Matthew 16:13–16; Luke 9:18–20.

2. John Calvin, *Institutes of the Christian Religion*, 2 vols., ed. John T. McNeil, trans. Ford Lewis Battles (Philadelphia: Westminster Press, 1960), 35.

3. This is a wonderful phrase from a traditional Irish wedding song, "Marie's Wedding."

4. The full saying goes, "Come to me, all who labor and are heavy laden, and I will give you rest" (Matthew 11:28).

5. James A. Michener, *Hawaii* (New York: Random House, 1959), 314–15.

6. John Calvin, *The Gospel According to St. John, Part I*, trans. T. H. L. Parker (Edinburgh: Oliver and Boyd, 1961; repr. Grand Rapids, Mich.: Eerdmans, 1980), 167.

7. This point of view is closely associated with Martin Luther's "theology of the cross," which is the prime example of God working "under contraries" to reveal Godself. A concise entry point on

this subject is Brian Gerrish, *The Old Protestantism and the New* (Chicago: University of Chicago Press, 1982), 132–34.

8. The earliest appearance of this phrase is in St. Ignatius's letter to the Ephesians. See *Early Christian Fathers*, ed. Cyril C. Richardson (New York: Macmillan, 1970), 93.

9. See Martin Luther, *Luther: Lecture on Romans*, ed. Wilhelm Pauck (Philadelphia: Westminster Press, 1961), 125.

10. C. S. Lewis, *Till We Have Faces: A Myth Retold* (1956; repr., New York: Harcourt Brace Jovanovich, 1980), 294. For a thorough study of what it may have meant to Lewis to "have a face," see Peter J. Schakel, *Reason and Imagination in C. S. Lewis: A Study of Till We Have Faces* (Grand Rapids, Mich.: Eerdmans, 1984), 78–86.

11. See Luke 22:44 for the description of Jesus at Gethsemane.

12. See *The Worshipbook: Services* (Philadelphia: Westminster Press, 1970), 45 (quoting 1 John 3:1).

13. "O Love, How Deep, How Broad, How High," attributed to Thomas à Kempis, can be found, among other places, in *The Presbyterian Hymnal* (Louisville: Westminster/John Knox Press, 1990), 83.

Chapter Four

THE MUSIC BREAKS

Is there no music that speaks of our terrible brokenness? That's not what I mean. I mean: Is there no music that *fits* our brokenness? The music that speaks about our brokenness is not itself broken. Is there no broken music?

— NICHOLAS WOLTERSTORFF, *Lament for a Son*[1]

You can survive on your own. You can grow strong on your own. You can even prevail on your own. But you cannot become human on your own.

— FREDERICK BUECHNER, *The Sacred Journey*[2]

Brownie said, "It was the wrists, dear. All that rocking back and forth — I suppose it acted like a pump. All over her dress, the rocker.... There wasn't a thing in the world you could do. 'Read me about Jesus, Brownie.' Those were her last words, dear. What a blessing to know she slipped away with the music of Scripture in her ears."

— FREDERICK BUECHNER, *The Book of Bebb*[3]

THE MOMENT OF DECISION was one of the few instances of perfect clarity in Bill's life. The trees stood out in surrealistic three-D, they were so clear. Bill remembered when he got his first pair of glasses at age ten. It was the leaves on the tree that amazed him most. He would sit and just stare at them. He could never have imagined before he got his glasses that you could make out individual leaves on a tree. And they were so clear, he would tell anyone who would listen to him. The trees around him were

clear in a brand new way, just as if he were putting on spiritual glasses, or mind glasses, or whatever you wanted to call
them. The world about him stood out and outlined itself in
perfectly bold strokes.

There was no hesitation in this moment of clarity. Of all
the crystal clear images about him, two struck his eyes open
in a way they had never been open before. One was the
road. Not the road that his car sat on; the road that was
calling him to follow. At first, the two roads ran contigu-
ously. But then the road of his vision, the road that led to
his destiny, ran straight where the asphalt road made a big
looping curve to the right. And standing at the end of the
road was a big, new, shiny metal streetlight. Bill was amazed
that the city's ponderous process of getting new street lights
so meshed with his own needs and personal vision. He was
sure this road, with its shiny metallic *telos,* was part of a
divine plan.

The light changed from red to green. Bill revved the engine, pushed the accelerator to the floor, and left it there.
From first to second gear, rpm's screamed from the engine. Second to third was smooth, engine still yelling "go!"
Bill looked up at the loopy curve, so crooked and pathetic
looking compared to his nice, straight road. No cars were
coming. Bill didn't want to hurt anyone. Four or five seconds since the starting line, since the greenlight to his future.
He deftly pulled down on the stick shift, going from third to
fourth. The car approached fifty miles per hour. Bill reached
down and unbuckled his seatbelt, calmly but firmly pushing
it next to the car door with his left hand. The final task ac-
complished, the left hand found its way back to the steering
wheel, freeing the right hand for the final gear shift to fifth.
Bill glanced at the speedometer — nearing seventy. He looked
up and laughed, the first real laugh of the last seven miser-
able hell-on-earth months. "All roads lead home!" he yelled.
The picture was so clear. Before the darkness, he could see
the front of the car buckle at the impact, and he held up

his hands to the windshield, extended as if to a long, lost lover, to meet the shattering glass, to caress its sharpness as he passed through it on his way to oblivion. The most perfectly clear moment of his life. Bill was glad that it was this moment that would be his last.

"Look, here's the opening scene for a novel," I said as I showed my closest friend the pages above that describe a suicide attempt. "It's called *Doors*. The guy is practically dead from the car wreck. Yet he wakes up in the hospital and thinks himself alive." My friend looked at me, uncertainty causing a wrinkling of the brow.

I tried to explain a bit more about the plot. How the guy would be in a double room, but the curtain was always pulled. There were two doorways, one through which the other man received visitors and one that admits the man's dead wife. She comes and talks to him, and they discuss all the important issues of life and all the good things they had done together. When his wife was not visiting, the man would lie there and listen to the conversations that surrounded his roommate. The roommate was in critical condition, not expected to live. The folks who came in through the hospital door carried on such petty arguments and mundane discussions that the man thought, "If that guy does make it through, what a hell of a life to come back to." Finally, after a few days, the man's wife comes and invites him to leave the hospital, following her through the supernatural door by which she comes and goes. He gladly goes. At that exact moment, the man in the other bed dies. They are, in fact, the same man.

I nervously waited for a response from my friend. And then she asked the question I both wanted with all my being to avoid and that I hoped beyond hope she would ask: "Is this about you?"

At that time, thoughts of suicide were coming to me more often than before. Several months before I showed this story to my friend, I had tried to articulate my feelings about suicide, how they would pop into my mind, at a bereavement group. It was a small group, and I don't think the person facilitating it had very much experience.

The immediate reaction from one person was, "You can't do that. How can you even think about it? You're a minister. Your wife was a minister. How can you even say that?"

Rather than coming to my rescue or at least aiding my halfhearted attempt at getting at what was for me a very serious situation, the facilitator said nothing. I was left to mutter something about it not really being serious and let it drop. I also never went back to that group.

Because of that experience, I was loath to share my feelings with anyone else. With grief comes a loss of self-confidence, and I did not feel confident enough to try to share my innermost thoughts with anyone, afraid I would be rejected, chastised, and embarrassed. If a stranger had so affected me, how would I cope with a friend giving me the same message? On the one hand, I should have known that friends and family would have at least tried to be more supportive than this group-therapy participant. On the other hand, I was afraid to risk it. I was afraid I'd lose their respect, afraid I would scare them, afraid they would think I was trying to get attention (which I needed), afraid they'd think me a man of little faith. That, above all else, is what I heard that night in group counseling — an indictment of my faith ("You're a minister. How can you think that?").

Little did that person know that faith was at the heart of my problem, but not in the way she might have meant it. She meant my lack of personal faith. Perhaps I did have a lack of personal faith, yet that was not the case. In fact, taking things in a different sense, the problem was too much faith. Though it may sound irrational, I felt that the weight of faith was about to crush me. The burden of faith — to be a faithful person, to live a faithful life, to share faith with my children — at times overwhelmed me. The faith that proclaimed

God's goodness and mercy was exactly what was troubling me. I believed, at an intellectual level, the promises of the gospel. I accepted, at the emotional level, the trust I had in those promises. Yet in my circumstances, that faith was not freeing. It was a weight on my chest, pressing down, ever down, and every gasp for breath meant a tightening, every breath exhaled meant more pressure. Faith was a boa constrictor, suffocating me. All air was breathed out; I could not breathe in.

I conceived of faith during these times as a duty: It was my duty to be a person of faith. As I tried to bear up under it alone, I felt more and more unable to carry the weight. Grief made my faith heavy. Bereavement left me in a state of solitude. It would obviously be inappropriate to share my struggles with my children. Many of my friends and family were hundreds of miles away, and my problem didn't seem like one that made for good phone chat. I was afraid what the revelation of my thoughts would do to my friends at hand, afraid of a radical change in relationship or the breaking of relationships.

I also labored under the absurd notion that an individual bears his or her duty alone, and it was my job to carry my own burdens. The burden was heavy; the yoke of Jesus didn't seem light. I was, I felt, expected to stand tall, as if faith were a pick-me-up pill that could be swallowed as a cure-all. I choked on it at times. Grief, the state of my bereavement, mixed up with some of my religious expectations of myself, felt mostly like suffocation. I was at the point I imagine would come with real suffocation, when you welcome the darkness that envelopes you and the unconscious state that surrounds you, just so you don't have to feeling the suffocating feeling anymore.

That was one of the things so appealing about thoughts of death — release from the suffocating weight that seemed to be on me. I was often tired, the pain of grief was real, and the loneliness sometimes struck me like a hard slap across the face. I could cope with all these things better than with the lack of air I seemed to experience. The seduction of suicidal thoughts was this: There's a simple way to throw off the weight. Death was the lens that lent clarity to my vision. The thoughts were seductive, like a lover. This surprised me. The knife that could cut my wrist became personified. After one particularly intense experience, I tried to write out what had happened.

> The curved blade of the knife smiles a sensuous smile,
> Its sharp tip a tongue, yearning to greet me with lover's kiss,
> To penetrate my mouth, my throat, my heart,
> To lie with me alone in intimate embrace.

> But I am an innocent, still devoted, still faithful,
> To the one who's past temptation's face,
> Yet I remain, alone, and afraid, and wondering,
> How to avoid the wiles of temptation's smile.

Every breath I breathed, it seemed, was a wish for Melanie; every intake of air brought the knife of grief. The circumstances seemed unbearable, and I could not bear the faith that so many people say makes such circumstances bearable.

If one of the appeals of suicide was release from the tremendous weight, so much so that suicide became seductively appealing, the other thing that contributed to more serious thoughts about suicide was Melanie's death itself. By her death, death became demystified for me. For someone like me, who had never seen someone die, just the experience of being there tore down the shrouds of mystery. I had seen someone die. What had been in many ways unthinkable was now thinkable. More to the point, death now seemed doable. I knew how it went, what the routine was. Death became an option because now, unlike before, it was a *real* option. Not a vague image of something with which I had no experience, death now presented itself as something I had, in a sense, lived through. What would have been the realm of fantasy became the realm of reality. It didn't take much imagination to imagine myself dead. All I had to do was pay attention to the picture of Melanie's death, which was never far removed from my consciousness.

The turning point came one afternoon. After thinking about it over and over again, after writing it up as the introduction to an idea for the so-called *Doors* novel, I found myself sitting at a red light. Just as in the story, I looked ahead, saw the metal streetlight pole, and for an awful instant, things became horrifyingly clear. As soon as the light turned green, I took off. I had just switched into fourth gear in my car. I was approaching 55 mph and was ready to shift into fifth. The road curved to the right as my track toward the pole took me straight ahead. Then, thank God, an image of my children came into my head. I hit the brakes, swerved back toward the curving road, pulled over, and brought the car to a stop. I started shaking. "What am I doing?" I kept asking myself over and over again.

The next day I went to the doctor, and I also discussed what had happened with my children's counselor. These two, along with my friend who read the *Doors* introduction, are the only people who ever knew how far my suicidal thoughts had gone.

For about a year or a year and a half after that, I visited the doctor fairly frequently. Though it became familiar, I never quite got used to the physician routinely asking me, "Tom, have you had any thoughts about killing yourself since we last talked?" What exactly did that mean? Was the doctor asking if I had driven at any trees lately? Did it mean fleeting thoughts of rest? Did it mean simply putting my body in the state that my soul already seemed to inhabit? These were good questions to ask, and the doctor kept them in my mind so I didn't slip off into death unthinkingly.

My children's counselor was the one who finally encouraged me to take myself seriously. If I had heard that a friend was talking and thinking the way I was, I would have immediately seen the utter seriousness of the situation. Yet I found it hard to do for myself. Taking my suicidal thoughts seriously meant that I had to take things into account that were a blow to my self-image. How depressed was I? Could I trust myself? Why couldn't I pull through this thing alone? Why wasn't I strong enough to snap out of my blue periods? What was wrong with my faith? Why wasn't my grasp on faith sufficient to pull me through this awful time? Why did religious words of comfort sound so hollow? These were hard questions to wrestle with, yet I had to, if I was going to take myself seriously.

I must admit, I chuckled as I thought back on some of my own experiences as a pastor, experiences that must be somewhat widely shared, because I ran across them in Reinhold Niebuhr's *Leaves from the Notebook of a Tamed Cynic.* Therein he recounts, as a freshly minted pastor, "I talk wisely about life and know little of life's problems."[4] I remembered sermons where I had talked of life's problems, of death and dying, suffering and grief. I thought they made for great rhetorical flourishes for my oral theologizing. How many times people who had experienced intense grief and pain must have thought of me contemptuously, "What does he know of these things?" Nothing. I knew nothing. The flashy smile, the rhetorical "God is love," and my smugness must have been resented by some because I came to resent that sort of approach as I worked through my own awful feelings of uncertainty, despair, and self-loathing. I could not, even with my faith, face the world without Melanie. Everything I lived for and proclaimed seemed to crumble in the face of my questioning. For the first time in my life, I had something to be dead serious about. I was a failure. I was broken, not whole; sinful, not right; sick, not healthy.

One cold winter day in Chicago, back in my graduate school days, after ice and snow had fallen, I was trudging through the wind on my way to work. Coming toward me was an old man, walking very slowly, very carefully. I started to slip right past him, the anonymity of the big-city street justification enough to ignore him, when his hand shot out and grabbed hold of my arm. His eyes held mine for a few seconds. His was an old face and, it appeared, a defeated face, one that would rather move away from life than toward it. Then he spoke. "My greatest fear in life," he said, "is falling." His voice broke as he said "falling." He shook his head.

"Can I help you get where you're going?" I asked him.

"No, no," he spoke slowly, seeming to be thinking as the words came out. "I'm going to fall sometime or another. If not now, later. But I'm just so afraid." Then he let go of my arm and shuffled on down the street.

I think everyone's greatest fear, when all is said and done, is falling. Though my fear was not of a physical fall, it was of a spiritual and emotional fall. To fall when we're alone and unable to get up is scary. When Melanie died, I not only lost my wife but my life's companion, the one who reached down to pull me up when I would fall. Now that I was falling into the darkest period of my life, I felt forsaken. Her hand was not there to lift me up. It seemed I was alone in the pit, alone in the darkness, alone with the many questions that sat like judges and condemned my life alone. "My God, my God, why have you forsaken me? Why has Melanie forsaken me? Why has my life forsaken me?"

This experience is both shared and unshared. Nicholas Wolterstorff, writing in *Lament for a Son*, speaks of the way that grief isolates,[5] and isolation is an aspect of forsakenness. Yes, we all at one time or another experience grief, but everyone's grief is different. It seems to put us in a category by ourselves, and the bridge from one person to another becomes almost impossible to cross at times. Even that which is most strongly evocative for us in terms of making connections and relationships in life can seem to fly apart when faced with grief at its fiercest.

What has often served as the emotional tie for me in the way I relate to the world is music. Yet at my lowest, in my deepest struggles, the music didn't seem to work anymore.

Can we hear the Lord's song when grief has made us tone deaf? That which I most relied on seemed to abandon me. Why didn't my spirit soar when I heard music that once had been able to shield me from my darkest moments? Wolterstorff, in an extraordinarily observant way, answered that for me when I read his *Lament for a Son*. For him, also, music is a balm. Yet when reaching a discordant place in his grief, he found that what he needed wasn't a whole music, because he wasn't whole. He needed broken music to reflect his broken state of soul.

I found this a powerful metaphor for my inner life, though I changed Wolterstorff's intent a bit. I wasn't looking for a broken music. In my mind, the music had already snapped, and the lyrics that came to my mind were from Don McLean's "American Pie," where he talks about going to the "sacred store" where he had heard the music before. But what he found was that the music wouldn't play. And McLean then speaks about silence — no words are spoken, church bells are broken — and then he ties that situation, that lack of music, to absence. Moreover, he does so in trinitarian terms — he says that Father, Son, and Holy Ghost, those he admired most, had a caught a train and left. And what was this moment, this "day," in McLean's song? It was "the day the music died."[6] Though I don't know how McLean meant these words to be taken, they were perfect in my own personal context. The broken music meant that God was gone. I no longer heard the strains of Zion, not even its slightest echo.

C. S. Lewis once remarked that "the trouble about God is that he is like a person who never acknowledges your letters and so in time you come to the conclusion that either he does not exist or that you have got his address wrong."[7] I have never doubted God's existence, even in my darkest moments. Though my faith might be suffocating or twisted in some way, it was still faith in a God out there. But the "wrong address" observation is pretty accurate. The right connection was not being made, and I was completely out of touch with God. To return to a musical metaphor, I was frantically searching the spiritual airwaves for the divine music that so often touched my soul with joy, but all I was able to tune in was static.

A number of things eventually helped me move out of my deadening spiritual malaise. All were important, though I can't rank them. I needed them all, and so, in no particular order of importance, these things helped move me out of my private hell, back into the world of God's light and life.

Important relationships shed grace on my life at a time when I seemed to have forgotten that life, true life, is not characterized by happiness or comfort or lack of pain. Neither is it characterized by sorrow or pain or bereavement. True life is characterized by love, and love is manifest only through relationships. Though my physical and temporal relationship with Melanie had ended, there were elements of it that remained and brought gladness: Mave and Gwynne, our children. Their image kept me from running into a pole at high speed.

Sometimes people speak and act as if love has no power or does not really matter in this gone-to-the-devil world of ours. That's not true. Love mattered to me that day. It was the line that separated me from nonbeing. Love makes connections, moving out in concentric circles, making life worth living. The girls are a concentric circle extending from Melanie. Her love was great; it is extended and continues in Mave and Gwynne, becoming more and greater than it was.

At the center of the pond of human existence, the eternal act of God revealing Godself in love through the Incarnation of Christ Jesus is the stone that has dropped from above, the cause of the ever-widening concentric circles of love. When I was at my lowest, most despairing, faced with drowning in sorrow in that pond of human existence — when I searched for and could not find God — the circle of love emanating from my children touched me. Because that love touched me,

I can look back and see the circle of Melanie's love. I can look even further back and see in her the act of God's love in Christ as the force that sustained her and formed her circle of love.

A friend's touch helped me immensely in my time of confusion and sorrow. I could not find God's address, so God found mine. He sent a letter carrier my way, an angel. *Angel* is, after all, a Greek word that means "messenger." Through this friend's touch, comfort, and words of hope and concern, God spoke to me. I didn't always hear or pay attention. I wasn't always aware of it. But God spoke to me often and extended comfort through my friend. Looking back, God's word was incarnate in my friend, holding my hand to comfort me when the simple words, "God holds your hand in times of sorrow" would not have meant anything to me. God's action was (and is) God's word.

Books were important to me. They attuned my ears to the music of grace when I was afraid all I would ever hear again was the noise of cacophonous despair. Reading moved me beyond myself, opened me to more than what I alone experienced in my moments of grief. In a lovely piece of writing for an academic audience, C. S. Lewis wrote in *An Experiment in Criticism* that "my own eyes are not enough for me.... In reading great literature.... I transcend myself; and I am never more myself than when I do."[8] If at times I was captive to what I felt, if grief imprisoned my soul so that I seemed nothing, small, and empty, then it was books, experiences, and well-turned phrases that were the key to unlocking my dungeon and setting my spirit free — not all at once, but often enough that despair did not win.

Some of the stunning insights of Frederick Buechner grew increasingly important for me. I believe this is so because of Buechner's own encounter with suicide: His father killed himself when Buechner was ten. This was an experience he had to face and fight much of his life. When Buechner writes of life and death, I listen. What's more, as the selection at the beginning of this chapter from *The Book of Bebb* shows, Buechner knows how intertwined our life-and-death decisions are with our Christianity. Even in the face of death, even in the willful embrace of death that was simply a running from living death, Christ figures in. "Read me about Jesus," Lucille asks her friend Brownie as her life blood flows from her. Rocking her life away, despair the seeming victor, there's still the hope of consolation. "Read me about Jesus."

Even in the face of a life that is no longer bearable, one wants to know that somewhere, somehow, someone has overcome the unbearableness of life to achieve an abundant life, a real, true life. "Read me about Jesus" is a request to hear of one who died yet was raised; who descended the depths of hell yet ascended the mountain of joy; who, walking through the very shadow of death itself, brought light to scatter the darkness. Though in language different from Scripture, different from formal theology, Buechner's books "read me about Jesus," and I listened.

At times the language of Scripture sounded too familiar to shake my malaise. I could only hear the words in the sugar-coated wrapping of shallow sermonizing. The words of theology seemed ripped from any mooring in honest-to-goodness grief-stricken life, but the language of imagination, Buechner's poetic prose, "read me about Jesus."

The one phrase that crystallized the images in my imagination is from *Godric*. In some ways, it is a simple phrase, but placed within the context of the book and Saint Godric's life — a real life full of joys and sorrows and sins and forgiveness — it held power. "All the death that ever was, set next to life, would scarcely fill a cup."[9] Reading those words, I realized that what I longed for was not death, but life. What I was living in was the loneliness of hell; death incarnate was my form. "All the death that ever was, set next to life, would scarcely fill a cup." In reading those words, I knew what my suicidal thoughts really meant: What I wanted more than anything else — the very desire of my heart — was not for life to end but for it to begin.

For me, Melanie embodied real life. Knowing her to be dead, I thought real life ended with her. Sometimes I wonder if she, like God, sits in the heavens and laughs at my foolishness. Perhaps it is a gentle laugh, because my mistake was birthed from such great pain. But mistake it was, nonetheless. If I had paid better attention to Melanie's life, and to the God who filled it with such meaning and joy, I would not have edged so close to the brink of destruction. Buechner's words pulled me back from the edge enough to be able to see Melanie's life, and the life God offers, for what it is: not something that is taken away or can even be thrown away, but a gift that continues now and forever, the having of it only requiring my accepting it.

Thank you, Frederick Buechner. Thank you, Mave and Gwynne. Thank you, Melanie. Thank you, special friend. Thank you, God, and thanks be to your son, Jesus Christ. Thank you all for not only helping me survive but also for helping me take steps toward becoming human, because I could not have done it alone. "Read me about Jesus." Read me about true life. Give me ears to hear, eyes to see, and hands to lift in praise.

Notes

1. Nicholas Wolterstorff, *Lament for a Son* (Grand Rapids, Mich.: Eerdmans, 1987), 52.

2. Frederick Buechner, *The Sacred Journey* (San Francisco: Harper and Row, 1982), 46.

3. Frederick Buechner, *The Book of Bebb* (New York: Atheneum, 1979), 243.

4. Reinhold Niebuhr, *Leaves from the Notebook of a Tamed Cynic* (1929; repr., Louisville: Westminster/John Knox Press, 1980), 9.

5. Wolterstorff, *Lament for a Son*, 56.

6. Don McLean, "American Pie" (New York: MCA Publishing, 1971).

7. C. S. Lewis, quoted in George Sayer, *Jack: A Life of C. S. Lewis* (Wheaton, Ill.: Crossway Books, 1994), 158.

8. C. S. Lewis, *The Essential C. S. Lewis,* ed. Lyle W. Dorsett (New York: Collier Books, 1988), 515.

9. Frederick Buechner, *Godric: A Novel* (New York: Atheneum, 1980), 96.

Chapter Five

PSYCHOPHARMACOLOGICAL CALVINISM

Now, among the Christians there are also new Stoics, who count it depraved not only to groan and weep but also to be sad and care ridden. . . . Yet we have nothing to do with this iron philosophy which our Lord and Master has condemned not only by his word, but also by his example. For he groaned and wept both over his own and others' misfortunes.

— JOHN CALVIN, *Institutes of the Christian Religion*[1]

My soul is very sorrowful, even to death.   — JESUS[2]

Have daylight mercy on my midnight soul.

— Godric's prayer, FREDERICK BUECHNER, *Godric*[3]

 MANY THINGS HELPED ME in my struggle to see through pain to life. Books and relationships — my relationship with people and my relationship with God (though that at times was a real struggle) — were blessed boons. These are things people can hear and relate to and find praiseworthy in some measure. Yes, it is right that your living relationships should pull you through. Yes, it is right for you (though not perhaps for everyone) that your reading should be a big help (though I can already hear the "tsk-tsk"-ing that straightforward Scripture isn't given more credit). But there is another thing I must credit with my turn toward life — Prozac. And here things become more complicated.

There is no doubt in my mind that this medicine was a

lifesaver for me. My physician prescribed it after my "vision" of embracing the light pole at high speed. I had been taking an antidepressant — my "sleeping medicine" as I euphemistically referred to it around the few people who knew I took medication — but it no longer seemed to be working. Not only was I experiencing suicidal thoughts, my sleep patterns had changed, and my "sleeping medicine" no longer made me sleep. My depression was getting worse, and the medicine was no longer combatting it as effectively as it had for the past few years. Prozac helped me sleep better, and it lifted my spirits. I needed both. It is the latter part of that sentence that becomes problematic when the language of Christianity is stirred into the mix. I was taking a drug to lift my spirit. Wasn't that faith's function? Implicitly, if I had to use a drug to lift my spirit, then there was a failure in my spiritual life, particularly my life of faith. At least that's how we can phrase the problem in order to explore it.

Is there a conflict between faith and mood-enhancing drugs? Is it a failure of faith to have one's spirit descend so low that it takes medication to lift it again? Our culture, despite the supposed triumph of the therapeutic, does not deal well with mental ailments, of which depression is one. In our culture, in those places where *faith* as a meaningful word no longer operates, there is still the notion of the rugged individual who copes through his or her own resources, pulls from within, reaches deep down and "sucks it up" in order to cope with bad times. Christian or not, large numbers of people think of mental problems, especially depression, as simply a failure of inner resolve and resources (whether this is faith or some secularized version of it doesn't matter).

Because of this widespread attitude, those of us who have had to take medication for depression often buy into this mind-set, which means we feel guilty for taking the drugs that make us not only feel better (which is a godsend, don't be fooled) but that also make us able to function normally and, in some cases, desire to continue living. In what is, for me — as a historian of Christian thought with a special interest in John Calvin — a delicious irony of sorts, there's a name for this guilt over taking drugs: psychopharmacological Calvinism.[4] That term is actually used to describe this mental anguish over taking drugs to relieve severe mental anguish. Break it down: psycho = having to do with the mind; pharmacological = having to do with drugs; and Calvinism = having to do with guilt. The words *Calvin* and *Calvinism* have come to be shorthand in American culture for a whole range of negative things, including guilt.[5] This is ironic because Calvin, who was very sick for much of his life, valued and took advantage of the best medical treatment available to him. Yet his name is now used to label guilt over medical treatment.

It is true that taking a medicine such as Prozac can make one feel guilty. This comes about in two ways: through what other people say, and what one (especially as one of Christian faith) says to oneself.

In some ways, I have never felt so sheepish as when I have been around other people who talk about folks on Prozac. In nearly all cases, these discussions have been negative — not in a consciously mean-spirited manner, but more along the lines of an unconscious feeling of being above "all that."

When I was taking Prozac and someone said something about the drug, I felt as if someone said his or her watch had been stolen, and at that moment I reached down in my pocket to discover a watch there. I felt I had done something wrong, something of which I should be ashamed. There were fears of reprisal, of accusation, of blame. Most of all, there was the fear that someone would say, "Look what you've done. You're bad." More than this feeling of shame and guilt, I felt like a child. I was being indirectly scolded by someone bigger, stronger, older, wiser, smarter, tougher than me. So I kept silence, hoping to hold on to respect on the outside, even though I felt I had lost it on the inside.

Despite all the negative feedback I began to pick up on

(I didn't begin to pay attention to these comments until I started taking medication), it didn't compare to my own inner feelings of failure and the diminution of my self-worth. I belittled myself for having to rely on a drug. Slogans from my youth, when doing the kind of enthusiastic Christian youth work I engaged in, kept coming back to me. Music I performed rang in my ears: "Natural High" was one of them. Jesus was a natural high; all the other things offered as a substitute for that high were artificial, evil, and shallow compared to Jesus. The music of my youth — that bright, pulsating, optimistic sounding of Christian faith that I had embraced and loved and grew up in — condemned me now. I needed an unnatural high, which meant Jesus must be missing.

In some ways, these feelings of guilt over my lack of faith had to do with a number of things, none of which necessarily involved harsh judgments on songs that meant to inspire, not tear down. The problems weren't with the songs but with the way guilt worked into my life and into unresolved issues related to Melanie.

If I were not depressed but thinking more sanely, or if I were thinking of this in relation to a friend instead of myself, I would never have even considered guilt. After being so depressed, taking medication to help overcome that depression, and talking on occasion with a counselor, I came to realize that guilt was dominating my life. In fact, I believe there was a real failure of faith in my life at this time, but it had nothing to do with the medication and everything to do with Melanie.

Simply put, I came to understand that the root of my problem was that I felt I had betrayed Melanie. I let her die. My faith couldn't move the mountain of finitude that cast its shadow upon her. I, as the living one, had betrayed the one who had passed away. I betrayed Melanie by letting her die. I was her protector, and I had failed her. This isn't meant to sound chauvinistic — the big strong man taking care of the weak woman. Melanie was also my strength, and I miss that sorely. This feeling came, in part, from her. On more than one occasion, she spoke of how I made her feel safe. I was her refuge. Yet, in the end, I had turned her out. I was not a refuge but only an observer, watching as death broke down the doors of the sanctuary of life and took Melanie.

I could not protect her. I could not give her one more breath of life. I could not grant a single beat of the heart. I could not grace her soul with one moment more of union with her worn-out body. I could do nothing, say nothing, be nothing that mattered in any way. I felt overwhelming guilt at this, almost as if someone had looked at me with reproach and said, "*He* let her die."

This guilt served as the foundation for all the other ways guilt ate away at my life. My mind was turned in on itself, searching for failure over the entire range of my life, so I could justly condemn myself — guilty on all counts. Did I do enough for my kids? No. Guilty. Did I pray enough? No. Guilty. Did I fulfill my gifts that God granted me, did I work hard enough at being the best I could be? No. Guilty. Was my faith enough to weather the worst storm of my life? No. Guilty. I trespassed on all counts; I met none of the standards I set for myself. Because I couldn't cope with such failure, I took medication to avoid the pain, to artificially lift me from the pit of guilt, which is another word for the pit of meaninglessness. Life contained no natural high.

Have you ever tried to get away from yourself? I imagine we all try to do this at times. To paraphrase St. Augustine, where can I go and not find myself there?[6] That was the problem for me. I wanted to be away from myself, away from the guilt I felt, freed from the burden of memory that weighed me down. I couldn't get away from believing that I had let Melanie down, so I went about trying to free myself by engaging in mindless activities, hoping that by fleeing my mind and self-consciousness I could flee the guilt locked inside.

I kept (or thought I kept) the guilt and pain away through the use of electronic media. I would watch late-night TV, mindlessly viewing the pains of others vulgarly portrayed on talk shows. I would play solitaire on my computer for hours at a time, from midnight until two or three in the morning. I would play until my head ached. I'd stare at the screen — that lifeless, mind-numbing screen — until my eyes were sore. Anything to keep from going to bed, where the most obvious thing of all was that I slept alone. My aloneness was the greatest reminder of my guilt.

My personal experience has been, in so many ways, a case study in good theology, bringing home to me how doctrine can ring so true. Guilt as a theological category is a result of our lack of faith in God's promises of forgiveness. In some ways, this is a great sin. We presume not to forgive ourselves, even for something that realistically we have absolutely no control over, while God offers to forgive us freely. We choose guilt, probably because we choose sin. Because that becomes the habit of our lives and sin is characterized by being turned in on ourselves,[7] we develop overblown notions of what we can in fact control. What part of us really thinks we can do anything to alter life and death? Yet we take on godlike responsibility, and when we fail we punish ourselves with all the vindictiveness of a petty, small god. We pay a heavy penalty for playing god in our own lives. The penalty is guilt.

Guilt is a vicious circle. My goal in numbing myself, what I wanted to achieve by running away from my inner voice, was relief from guilt, release from the pain it caused. Yet in the very achievement of that goal — at those moments I thought I had clearly anesthetized myself to the pain — came greater pain. Though it may not make much sense rationally, on an emotional level it turned out that the greatest pain of all came when I recognized that I had attained a state of painlessness. Computer solitaire did in fact numb my senses enough that no pain was present — or at least no conscious pain about a conscious event. But in the very moment of attaining this state, I would realize that my lack of pain was a lack of humanity and a lack of love. It felt like the ultimate act of turning my back on Melanie. That which I sought, I got, but the fruit was bitter, worse than the original pain or guilt. Feeling guilty over experiencing a lack of guilt was a dead-end road, and that meant for me a dead-end life.

Because psychopharmacological Calvinism pervades the culture, I experienced guilt over relying on medicine. Yet it lifted me out of my own downtrodden spirit enough that I could start to cope with some of the issues that weren't drug or physiologically related (depression is a physiological state). In other words, though contributing to my guilt, the medication helped me escape from the grasp of depression long enough to begin to think through issues of faith and guilt, life and death, responsibility and gift.

I was able to come to the realization that much of the guilt I experienced over my seeming lack of faith was because I had inadvertently accepted some of the easy assumptions about faith that, in stronger moments, I would have rejected out of hand. The biggest of these assumptions is that faith makes one happy. Faith brings joy; faith carries satisfaction; faith bestows a type of blessedness; faith brings God's peace. But none of these are the same as "being happy," at least not in the sense in which that word is normally used.

In an extraordinary song often sung by youth choirs, William Alexander Percy paints a picture of life as a Christian. For all its sing-along melody, the song's lyrics are quite stern: God's peace and "happiness" are not the same thing. "They Cast Their Nets in Galilee" portrays a life of discipleship full of suffering. In a set of stunning lines, the song declares:

> Contented, peaceful fishermen,
> Before they ever knew
> The Peace of God that filled their hearts
> Brimfull, and broke them too.

> The Peace of God it is no peace
> But strife closed in the sod.
> Yet, brothers, pray for just one thing,
> the marvelous peace of God.[8]

Part of what this song is about, I think, is the recognition that the Christian life has a purpose, and the direct purpose of that life is not happiness but service to God.[9] We are not created for ourselves, but for another: "Our heart is restless, until it repose in thee," Saint Augustine said.[10] We are created to live to God's glory. That is our purpose. The classic Protestant reformers, especially John Calvin, knew this well. Happiness comes through the fulfilling of our purpose to glorify God.[11] In so much of American Christianity, the order of things has been reversed. We judge God according to our happiness. Whether or not we are happy determines God's glory and goodness. Yet that approach is neither biblical nor reformed. It is in our proper relationship to God, as one of God's creatures who gives God glory, to whom we owe the proper object of our love, that we find happiness. It is a hard lesson that is learned only in the living of it, but it is true, and we forget it. That is why theodicy — arguments for both God's existence and God's goodness in the light of the world's suffering — is so hard to articulate these days. God's goodness is judged by whether or not we are happy. But no theodicy will work whose image of God is that God's ultimate purpose is, bluntly, to make me happy.

If faith is not about God making me happy in trying circumstances, what is it about? If it is not a talisman to ward off unhappiness or protect us from the buffeting winds of life, what is it? I think George MacDonald, that nineteenth-century writer whose work "baptized" C. S. Lewis's imagination,[12] has something of use to tell us. In a letter to his father, MacDonald mused,

> a thousand times too much is said about faith.... I would never speak about faith, but speak about the Lord himself —
> not theologically, as to the why and wherefore of his death —

but as he showed himself in his life on earth, full of grace, love, beauty, tenderness and truth. Then the needy heart cannot help hoping and trusting in him, and having faith, without ever thinking about faith.[13]

Whereas I cannot wholly go along with MacDonald's desire to do away with theology or explanations of the atonement, for the person in grief struggling with faith, there is good advice here: Speak not about faith (a word that can be rather generic and substantially empty) but of Christ and his actions. MacDonald reminds us that faith, in and of itself, considered as a quality, a concept for reflection and speech, or a state of mind, is in fact rather useless. Faith is a means, not an end. Faith is not an attitude that I am able to hold and control, nor is it a toughness of mind that fulfills anything in and of itself. Faith, simply put, cannot bring happiness because that is not its function. At its barest, faith is a looking upon Jesus and thereby recognizing our need for something more than what we are by ourselves and trusting that by looking on him we gain what we need.

If we look at Jesus' life, as MacDonald counsels, what do we find? An involvement with life in all its messiness. Confrontations with despair, anger, guilt. Death looked in the face. Suffering freely taken on. Fear of horrible circumstances ("Father... remove this cup from me") and feelings of abandonment in the face of it all ("My God, my God, why hast thou forsaken me?").[14] A cross stands in the middle of Christianity, and this fact sweeps away any notion that Christian faith is nothing more than a positive attitude that brings a happy state of mind. To look at Jesus is faith, and if one looks, one can not be led astray for long by pie-in-the-sky claims of a life free of trouble, a notion of faith for faith's sake as a therapeutic balm for the troubling circumstances of life.

If faith is about Jesus, then it is about teeth-gritting determination in the face of the forces of destruction, being touched by those forces, at times seeming to be overwhelmed by those forces. If faith is about Jesus and not a feel-good remedy for what ails you, then it is through the very struggles of life, not the happy-go-lucky avoidance of pain and suffering, that faith proclaims "Risen!" It is, after all, from death itself that Jesus is raised, and *risen* is a word that resonates with joy, blessedness, and fulfillment. It can even resonate with happiness, as long as we never again associate that word with the devices and desires of our own hearts but with the power of God to raise life in the midst of death. As long as we are the objects of our own happiness, we will never truly be happy in the deepest Christian sense. When God becomes the object of our happiness, then we will be happy indeed. This is the struggle; this is the call; this is the road of discipleship.

This may seem rather convoluted, but convoluted probably is not the right word. It is more like *involved*. This is an involved understanding of faith. Granted, some folks don't like involved understandings of Christianity. They think it should be simple. On one level, it is: Confess the gospel and you shall be saved, Paul proclaims.[15] It sounds so simple. Yet an analysis of the words and concepts reveals that there is a depth there that can never be exhausted in this lifetime, for as we grow in Christian life, the notions of faith, gospel, salvation, Christ, and self grow as well. As C. S. Lewis noted in one of the more memorable lines from *Mere Christianity*, "It is no good asking for a simple religion. After all, real things are not simple. . . . The problem is not simple and the answer is not going to be simple either."[16] Real life is not simple.

Faith, properly understood, doesn't sweep away the involvement of Christian life but underscores it. Why? Because simplicity, at its most bare bone, is a matter of "what you see is what you get." Most common-sense philosophies of life, in the broad sense of how that is perceived in American culture, has this at its core: Trust your senses. Seeing is believing. Things are as they appear. Faith is the complete opposite of that point of view. Hebrews 11:1, in one of the most succinct and well-known definitions of faith, states that "faith is the assurance of things hoped for, the conviction of things not seen." John Calvin's reflection on this passage seems especially appropriate to highlight the tension that faith brings to lived experience:

> Thus our apostle teaches us that we do not have faith in God from things present but from the expectation of things still to come. The appearance of this contradiction is not without its charm. He says that faith is the substance, that is, the prop or the foundation on which we place our feet; but of what? Of things absent which are so far from being under our feet that they far exceed the power of our understanding to capture.
>
> The same idea runs through the second clause where he calls faith the evidence, that is the demonstration of things not seen. A demonstration makes things appear, and commonly refers only to what is subject to our senses. These two things apparently contradict each other, but yet they agree perfectly when we are concerned with faith. The Spirit of God shows us hidden things, the knowledge of which cannot reach our senses. Eternal life is promised to us, but it is promised to the dead; we are told of the resurrection of the blessed, but meantime we are involved in corruption; we are declared to be just, and sin dwells within us; we hear that we are blessed, but meantime we are overwhelmed by untold miseries; we are promised an abundance of all good things, but we are often hungry and thirsty; God proclaims that he will come to us immediately, but seems to be deaf to our cries. What would happen to us if we did not rely on our hope, and if our minds did not emerge above the world out of the midst of darkness through the shining Word of God and by His Spirit. Faith is therefore rightly called the substance of things which are still the objects of hope and the evidence of things not seen.[17]

This is an eloquent explanation of faith because: (a) it doesn't see faith as a rubber-stamp guarantee of present happiness — it is realistic in the discrepancies we experience between what God promises and what we actually seem to get at times; (b) it anchors faith in the work of God's Spirit, not in an individual's attitude toward life; (c) it is future oriented, so it can pull one forward rather than leaving one trapped by what is in one's past.

Though the title of this chapter is "Psychopharmacological Calvinism" and it started with reflections on taking antidepressants, it is really a chapter on the basic Christian issues of guilt and faith. The whole problem with taking Prozac was a chance for me to reflect on what was at the root of my guilt over taking medicine. In reflecting on these bigger issues, however, I can now address both the symptom and the cause — the medication and the guilt. Calvin has been good to read in the context of the issues of this chapter, because now I am convinced that (a) if Calvin were living today, he would have seen Prozac for what it is: in certain cases of clinical depression, an altogether fitting form of medical treatment; (b) Calvin would have recognized the underlying problem in my guilt complex, understood the struggles of faith in such a situation, and given words of comfort as a fellow struggler and participant in life's hardships. He would have counseled me that my faith would be entirely inadequate as long as it remained a product of my attitude on life. But faith, as a looking toward Christ — not trust in my own ability but trusting in Christ's mercy — would have salved my own conscience and the guilt I felt for not having enough faith. Of course I did not have enough faith, he would have said. It is not humanly possible to have enough faith in God; faith itself is a work of God.

Nothing illustrates faith better than the Lord's Supper. With a little bit of grape juice and a nibble of bread, Christians in my tradition proclaim, "Friends: This is the joyful feast of the people of God!"[18] There is no feast; only a God who promises feast. The only way to approach the table, according to Calvin, is in faith, which, according to the very first edition of Calvin's *Institutes*, reposes all things in God, but nothing in ourselves. "All the delights of the gospel," Calvin tells us, are set before us at the Lord's table.[19] God promises; faith, in spite of all circumstances and in spite of our own weakness, apprehends; it is left to us to lift up sacrifices of thanksgiving and praise. Here indeed is daylight mercy for a midnight soul.

God has preserved my life through his Word, through the hands of friends, through God's wisdom in the writings of God's children, and through a medicine devised by the rational mind that was placed within humanity. The greatest comfort of all is that, having survived a crisis of faith with all the help I could get, I know that God will continue to preserve me, not only now but forever. And God will not only preserve me but also complete my joy by satisfying the longing of my heart to rest completely in God.

Notes

1. John Calvin, *Institutes of the Christian Religion*, 2 vols., ed. John T. McNeil, trans. Ford Lewis Battles (Philadelphia: Westminster Press, 1960), 709.
2. Matthew 26:38; Mark 14:34.
3. Frederick Buechner, *Godric: A Novel* (New York: Atheneum, 1980), 140.
4. See, for example, Peter D. Kramer, *Listening to Prozac* (New York: Viking, 1993), 259.
5. See my article, "Images of Intolerance: John Calvin in Nineteenth-Century History Textbooks," *Church History* 65, no. 2 (June 1996): 234.
6. St. Augustine, *The Confessions of Saint Augustine*, trans. Edward B. Pusey (New York: Collier Books, 1961), 55.
7. This is Martin Luther's definition of sin. See the discussion in George Rupp, *The Righteousness of God: Luther Studies* (London: Hodder and Stoughton, 1953), 165.
8. William Alexander Percy, "They Cast Their Nets in Galilee," 1924.
9. In *Godric*, Buechner describes a scene in which Godric has a vision of John the Baptist, who says this to the saint: "Seek not saints to ease thy spirit's pain that thou mayest better serve. Thy pain's itself thy service. Godric, burn for God" (*Godric*, 143).
10. Augustine, *Confessions*, 11.

11. See *John Calvin: Selections from His Writings*, ed. John Dillenberger (Missoula, Mont.: Scholars Press, 1975), 249.

12. C. S. Lewis, *Surprised by Joy: The Shape of My Early Life* (San Diego: Harvest/HBJ, 1955), 181.

13. George MacDonald, *An Expression of Character: The Letters of George MacDonald*, ed. Glenn Edward Sadler (Grand Rapids, Mich.: Eerdmans, 1994), 84.

14. Mark 14:36; 15:34.

15. Romans 10:9.

16. Lewis, *The Essential C. S. Lewis*, 312.

17. John Calvin, *Commentary on Hebrews and 1 and 2 Peter*, trans. W. B. Johnston (Edinburgh: Oliver and Boyd, 1963; repr., Grand Rapids, Mich.: Eerdmans, 1980), 157–58.

18. *The Worshipbook*, 34.

19. Calvin, *Institutes*, 111.

Chapter Six

HOUSE OF MEMORIES

It is the joys once shared that have the stings. — C. S. Lewis[1]

Legolas: "But you have not forsaken your companions, and the least reward that you shall have is that the memory of Lothlorien shall remain ever clear and unstained in your heart, and shall neither fade nor grow stale."

Gimli: "Maybe, and I thank you for your words. True words doubtless; yet all such comfort is cold. Memory is not what the heart desires. That is only a mirror.... Elves may see things otherwise. Indeed I have heard that for them memory is more like to the waking world than to a dream. Not so for dwarves." — J. R. R. Tolkien, *The Fellowship of the Ring*[2]

For better or worse, I am more dwarf than elf. — TJD

 RECENT DISCUSSIONS OF MEMORY seem to me to miss the point. There is so much talk of the brain's physiology that memory itself, as an experience, seems reduced to an afterthought. One of the insights of C. S. Lewis, in one of his Narnia stories, is that what a thing is and what a thing is made of are different; the one cannot be reduced to the other.[3] Though the brain's chemistry may be less mysterious than before, the relation of our memory to ourselves remains, in some ways, a great mystery. One cannot speak of memory, even the grief-stricken memory, in relation to faith and God without turning to that font of Western Christian thought, St. Augustine.

In his *Confessions*, book ten, Augustine sings memory, the

notes shaping emotions we have of memory. He creates a beautifully poetic account of memory that, though not physiologically accurate, is certainly closer to what memory is to us existentially than any cold description of synapses could ever be. What a thing is and what a thing is made of are two different things.

> I come to the fields and spacious palaces of my memory, where are the treasures of innumerable images, brought into it from things of all sorts perceived by the senses....I can produce colours....And though my tongue be still, and my throat mute, so can I sing as much as I will....[O]ther things, piled in and up by the senses, I recall at my pleasure. Yea, I discern the breath of lilies from violets, though smelling nothing; and I prefer honey to sweet wine, smooth before rugged, at the time neither tasting nor handling, but remembering only....These things do I within, in the vast court of my memory....[Finally, addressing God] And how shall I find thee, if I remember thee not?[4]

The interesting thing to take from Augustine is that when he speaks about memory and its power, when he paints the halls of remembrance and sings the tune of recollection, he is not — and this is important — *not* speaking of the past! Memory has to do with the present.

In the strict sense of the word, for Augustine, time is experienced by the individual only in the present. Or, as Jaroslav Pelikan says in his study of time and memory in Augustine, "It is not accurate to speak of past, present, and future as 'three times' at all. The three times [are, for Augustine]: a time present of things past; a time present of things present; and a time present of things future" (in other words, memory, direct experience, and expectation).[5] When this is related to memory, it makes clear the implications of Augustine's notion that the affections of the mind are kept in the memory, but they are not experienced in the same way through memory that they are in direct experience. As Augustine says, "For without rejoicing I remember myself to have joyed; and without sorrow recollect my past sorrow....Sometimes, on the contrary, with joy do I remember my fore-past sorrow, and with sorrow, joy."[6] What controls my experience of "a time present of things past," that is, my memories, is my grief. And that is a grief unto itself. In some ways, it seems a sin to feel such sorrow at remembering my past life with Melanie. Ours was a good and wonderful life. It deserves to be remembered well and wonderfully. Yet I cannot. Grief is the thundercloud of my memory, casting shadow over the playful landscape of times past that were joyful, turning gray the colors of the field of memories. That is what hurts the most, and it is that to which C. S. Lewis was referring when he wrote, "It is the joys once shared that have the stings."

Sometimes I wonder if a person who has not experienced an overwhelming loss and a tremendous sense of grief can understand Lewis here. One expects the sorrowful times to bring sorrow, though Augustine speaks of how sorrowful times can be thought of joyfully, and perhaps I will one day reach that state. But the now I occupy doesn't allow for that. The sorrowful times my memory sings to me like a dirge. They hurt. Melanie's ravaged flesh shocks me; my children's reaction to the news of their mom's death rocks me; the wishing for God to intervene and save — to physically save that wonderfully physical person Melanie — is still a wish that quietly fills every room through which I move in the mansion of memory. This all seems normal, I think.

But the joys — it is the joys that hurt so much. Visiting my old seminary campus a while back, I stood in front of the library. Vividly I remembered picking up fallen branches from a nearby tree, tossing one to Melanie, and shouting "en garde." There we were, two seminary students in our twenties, parrying away in broad daylight like children, finally collapsing to the ground in laughter. It was as if someone had taken the sticks with which we had had our swordplay, bound them together into a stake, and driven them into my heart. It is the joys remembered that have the stings.

Not long ago, I stood at the front of a chapel at a wedding rehearsal. A young woman, who was only a child when Melanie first pastored the church she attended, was getting married. She had been our first daughter's baby-sitter. I had been included in the wedding as an officiant in celebration of Melanie's memory. It was all lovely until the pianist began to play one of the pieces for the prelude. As "Jesu, Joy of Man's Desiring" echoed in that sacred space, my heart stopped. Melanie had walked down the aisle of the church at our wedding to that piece of music. Her mom has an enlarged portrait of that moment. Joy indeed radiated from Melanie's face, a sweet smile looking for all the world like it was about to break open into a sweeter laughter. But as I heard the music at the rehearsal, it was like nails down a chalkboard. I flinched, put my hands up to protect my ears momentarily, and tears welled up in my eyes. I quietly walked out of the sanctuary into a side area, wiped my eyes, and steeled myself to the noise that once sounded so beautiful. "I won't let my feelings ruin this moment for them," I thought of the bride and groom to be. But it was hard. It is the joys remembered that have the stings.

I remember from my youth a song called "Days of Future Past." There are nights when I go to bed, the memories of Melanie there beside me so strong, and I remember the good times. But they bring no comfort, for time collapses in on me, and indeed there is no time of past, present, and future. It is all one. My current grief not only remembers with sadness the good times gone by, but that grief is compounded by the sense of "Days of Future Past," that is, a remembering of a time when I anticipated a future together with Melanie. Yet her death has caused those anticipations to pass away into the past before ever coming to be. In this present moment, I grieve not only for what was but also for what will not be. My memory calls up a future that once was but now is gone. When time collapses in this way for me, I feel as if I am the one that Augustine was describing when he described the damned: "never living, never dead, but end-lessly dying."[7] It is, indeed, the joys remembered—real joys remembered from the past, imagined joys that anticipated a future—that sting.

The pain is still so real: the pain of the bad things, the pain of the good. Though I, as Tolkien's Company of the Ring, have walked through my own personal Lothlorien, a place of beauty and good, it is cold and distant, as Gimli the Dwarf remarked to his friend Legolas the Elf. The question is, how do I live in such a state?

It is here that we turn again to Augustine's insight, for it is not only the sensible that resides in the memory, and it is not only my grief that controls its operation. God also resides there. "How shall I find thee, if I remember thee not?" Augustine asked.[8] If at times I cannot experience God's presence and grace directly, I can explore my memory and recall God and God's work, and I can take down from the shelves of remembrance times of faith. Those times are not just dead memories hidden in a past that cannot be recovered. They exist at the moment of my recollection in the present: a time present of things past, as Augustine said.

Here is where memory can be a two-edged sword or, to switch metaphors, an anchor. It is the joys remembered that have the stings. Here is an anchor that, at times, I am tied to, and it carries me down to the depths where I do not want to be, where I cannot breathe, where the pressure is so great I think my lungs will burst. But to remember God is also to have an anchor that secures the ship of my life. When day seems done, when I can no longer brave the waters, when it is too dark or too stormy to traverse the seas, an anchor keeps me in place. I may not move forward, but at least I am not lost. Faith remembered may not be able to propel me through my present, but it can at least make the present bearable until this present itself passes and faith and God become more than memories. Until that day in which I can grasp God's hand firmly in faith, I can remember the days of being held by God's love. Most days, that is enough, if I can just remember.

There is, in fact, perhaps a hidden power here, a power to protect and to save. William Faulkner, in a memorable line from his *Light in August*, commented, "Memory believes before knowing remembers."[9] Perhaps the knowledge of God that resides in memory hovers there, like the creative spirit of God brooding over the chaos before the moment of creation in Genesis, a potent but latent force that remains silent until God proclaims "Light" and light explodes into being. When I find God in memory or God calls out to me from the recesses of my memory, there is in that memory a knowledge of power that can re-create me that is kept safe there until my knowing — my attempts at thinking things through — finally gets around to remembering what has been there all along.

The Bible itself is chock full of references to memory and remembering, and most of them have to do with power and salvation. There are the numerous prayers to God that cry, Remember me! "[A]ccording to thy steadfast love remember me, for thy goodness' sake, O Lord!" reads Psalm 25:7. Later, at Psalm 106:4, there is this: "Remember me, O Lord, when thou showest favor to thy people; help me when thou deliverest them." In that cry is the expectation that when God remembers us, God saves us. When asking God, as the psalmist does, to remember not my transgressions, I am asking God to remember the good that is in me and forget what is evil. As a Christian, I believe that what God remembers as good in me is the work of Christ, so that in God's own memory my sinful nature fades away, to be replaced by the image of Christ. In that recollection I am remade.

Perhaps the call is reciprocal. If God is to remember good, then as God's children we are to mirror God's actions. We too are to remember the good, which is to remember God. The psalms are full of admonitions to remember God "and forget not all his benefits" (Psalm 103:2). As the image of God, we as humans and Christians can scan our memories for pictures of the work of Christ and therein remember the good that is God. If the Christ on the cross in the recesses of memory becomes our Christ, if the revelation of divine love becomes a message for us, then we indeed come to remember that we are children of God, beloved and sanctified by God. There is no other real God, Luther reminded his readers, than God for us.[10] All others, no matter how rationally satisfying, are shams, for in the end they make no difference to us. God up in heaven, apart from the struggles and trials through which we fight in life, may be a nice idea, but God in practice is the God for us, one who takes on flesh, one who suffers and dies, so that the sense of our suffering and weakness is taken up into Godhood, to be remembered by God. Remember us, O God, and help us to remember you.

It all sounds so simple, but it is so hard. Only by remembering the good that is God do memories characterized by regret become memories of celebration. That is the task of the Christian in grief, when bereavement cuts so sharp and deep even memory itself is shredded. As hard as this is, though, it may be the price of not only our humanity but also of our connection to God. Perhaps we hurt so much because we are like God in some way, created in God's image — hurt so much that even the good and joyful of the past becomes blurred with agony in the present situation of loss. Maybe that hurt is what leads God to an incarnation — to hurt even more so that, finally, the hurt may heal and become health again. There is a price to be paid for being created in God's image, as C. S. Lewis poetically reminds us:

> That we, though small might quiver with Fire's same
> Substantial form as Thou — not reflect merely
> Like lunar angels back to Thee cold flame.
> Gods are we, Thou has said; and we pay dearly.[11]

Memory, at least for a time, exacts that price.

I see all the things that remind me of Melanie, and it hurts that those physical tokens can remind me of Melanie without recalling the joy that accompanied those things. I occasionally look at her diploma, a Doctor of Ministry degree that she labored on for five years while juggling the responsibilities of pastorate, motherhood, and being a wife. There was joy at its completion, a future of continued ministry. She was an excellent minister, one who entered the lives of those who called her pastor. Now all the diploma represents is a cold piece of paper that is witness to a future remembered but not lived. I look at the crewel embroidery she stitched for the children — playful kittens and mom, with a lazy but happy attitude toward life; a little girl with a basket of beautiful flowers, enjoying the day as the day gives itself to be enjoyed. But now there are no happy lazy days with Melanie, and there are no more days giving themselves up to be enjoyed in leisured beauty.

I see Wilbur the pig, who accompanied Melanie into the sanitized environment of the leukemia ward, where a clear plastic curtain separated her from death-mongering germs. Wilbur sat just outside the curtain, next to her bed. Now Wilbur sits in my children's room; no plastic curtain, but no Melanie, either. Material objects, present to my senses, scream of her absence.

Even worse is what's inside all of us who miss her so badly. Nearly five years after Melanie's death, the children occasionally fall to sleep crying over and over, "I miss my mommy." Both have woken up from dreams early in the morning, and their first word coming out of the hazy dreamscape of their minds is "Mommy!" When my first book came out, I stood there with it in my hands, and my first impulse was to turn and say, "Melanie, look!" Melanie believed in me as a writer, even for those many years when I wrote hardly a word. Now four books have been written, and she saw none of them in print. If it is the joys once shared that have the stings, it is also true that the joys that can no longer be shared also sting.

What we all remember and miss is the "old" us — the

old family — all of us together. Sharing in joys and sorrows, good times and not so great times, but always sharing. It was, looking back, an innocent time, one devoid of any real knowledge of mortality. I once wrote in a journal after Melanie's death, "I miss me, the old me, the laughing, innocent, sure-of-the-world me." I am gone, and only memories of the old me remain. Perhaps that is why so often even the good memories bring only sorrow. They seem so detached from me that I am not even sure I can claim them as "my" memories. They are the old Tom's memories, the man who didn't cringe in the face of death. I am so overwhelmed sometimes by the news I hear of the many and multiple and collective deaths, some of them horrific, going on in the world. The pain multiplies in a way it could not have before; I am more empathetic to what the survivors must feel. Whole cultures, it seems, are dying.

Memory of past things rampant with the pain of the present — that is the situation that must be addressed somehow. And yet, finally, as Augustine knew, since God is in memory, God somehow sustains. God sustains because God remembers us. God remembers our pain because God remembers a cross and a loss. I remember God through my pain, as well. Perhaps the cross connects humanity and God in ways we as Christians have not explored enough.

While I was visiting with some folks who had once been Melanie's parishioners, one of them remarked, "Melanie was a real person, you know. So full of life. That doesn't go away." The comment made me think, "What is it that was (is) real about Melanie?" As I thought back on her life, remembered who she was, I think I began to understand.

George MacDonald once wrote to his stepmother, "There is no gift so good, but its chief goodness is that God gives it, and what he gives is not to be taken away again."[12] Melanie's life was a gift. What was most real about her, what made her that real person, was that she knew life was a gift — not just after she was sick, but before as well. She embraced life;

she embraced the gift God had given. She embraced herself as God's own and all others as well. In other words, in her lived existence, she exemplified what it is that characterizes, at heart, all existence: the gifted nature of life. God gives, we receive. The simple acknowledgment of that relationship is the cornerstone to understanding the nature of existence. Even death cannot nullify the nature of God to give. Even death cannot nullify Melanie's own grace: to joyfully receive what is given. Death does not take away the gift of life; it simply underscores its giftedness.

Living in the state of this grace is what made Melanie real. Her life embodied the insight that Frederick Buechner has written in such heart-touching words in his historical fiction, *Godric*. When Godric reflects that "What's lost is nothing to what's found, and all the death that ever was, set next to life, would scarcely fill a cup,"[13] I think he is pointing to the gift nature of true life. So why is death so hard for us, beyond the obvious reasons of hurt and pain and grief? Because we forget that life is a gift, not a right. We exist under pure grace and for no other reason. If we trust God's memory, we know God will not forget us or our loved ones in life or in death, for that is God's nature. God hasn't taken away the gift of Melanie; it has been preserved for all eternity.

The joys still sting. Perhaps while I am in this life they always will. Like Tolkien's dwarf, my memory is not great enough to bring Melanie to life, so remembering her is not the same as having her. Maybe that itself is the very source of the stings. But the Christian's job in faith is not to excise grief but to simply remember that the God who gives such good as the gift of life can be trusted.

In *The Dark Is Rising*, Susan Cooper writes a remarkable series based on the King Arthur legends. A person named Merriman represents the figure of Merlin. He also represents a supernatural force of good in the world. After a battle, a man named Hawkin is thrown from the sky by the forces of evil. He is a man that evil had used and then, when the battle was lost, simply discarded.

Hawkin once served Merriman, but in an event in which Hawkin thought Merriman had endangered his life, he turned from Merriman to the dark side. For hundreds of years, Hawkin had nursed memories of betrayal. He was not able to remember the good in his relationship with Merriman but only saw the one dark moment. At the end of the book, Hawkin lay at Merriman's feet, a broken man with broken memories.

In one of the most moving and profound scenes in children's fiction, Merriman reminds Hawkin that Hawkin always could have turned back to the light, even at the moment of death. Hawkin thinks for a moment, and a change comes over his face. He looks up at Merriman with the look of remembrance — remembering himself, remembering who Merriman was, remembering their relationship — and he says, with final peace, "Master!"[14] He lays down his life of despair for a death of comfort, because in that moment he realizes wherein true life lies.

Though hard at times, though blurry because of tears and sorrow, when I remember that I, too, have a Master, peace comes. Not perfectly. Not completely. That will come. As long as I realize that God sits as the foundation for my house of memories, I know that it can be, over time, restored, so that it is no longer a gray and dilapidated jury-rigged wreck, but a house of beauty and comfort. More than a house — a home.

Notes

1. C. S. Lewis, "Joys That Sting," in Lewis, *The Essential C. S. Lewis*, 420.

2. J. R. R. Tolkien, *The Lord of the Rings*, part 1: *The Fellowship of the Ring* (New York: Ballantine Books, 1965), 490.

3. C. S. Lewis, *The Voyage of the Dawn Treader* (New York: Macmillan, 1952), 175.

4. Augustine, *Confessions*, 158–66.

5. Jaroslav Pelikan, *The Mystery of Continuity: Time and History, Memory and Eternity in the Thought of Saint Augustine* (Charlottesville: University Press of Virginia, 1986), 27.

6. Augustine, *Confessions*, 162.

7. Augustine, cited in Pelikan, *Mystery of Continuity*, 33.

8. Augustine, *Confessions*, 166.

9. William Faulkner, *Light in August* (New York: Random House, 1950), 104.

10. "The words OUR, US, FOR US, ought to be written in golden letters — the man who does not believe them is not a Christian." Martin Luther, cited in Timothy George, *The Theology of the Reformers* (Nashville, Tenn.: Broadman, 1988), 60.

11. C. S. Lewis, "Scazons," in Lewis, *The Essential C. S. Lewis*, 421.

12. MacDonald, *An Expression of Character*, 129.

13. Buechner, *Godric*, 96.

14. Susan Cooper, *The Dark Is Rising* (New York: Atheneum, 1977), 203.

Chapter Seven

WORDS OF GOOD COUNSEL

And God said, "Let there be light"; and there was light.

—Genesis 1:3

In the beginning was the Word, and the Word was with God, and the Word was God. He was in the beginning with God; all things were made through him, and without him was not anything made that was made. —John 1:1–3

This expression is indeed remarkable... that through His speaking God makes something out of nothing.... Therefore in the beginning and before every creature there is the Word, and it is such a powerful Word that it makes all things out of nothing.... Paul regards the conversion of the wicked — something which is also brought about by the Word — as a new work of creation.

—MARTIN LUTHER, *Commentary on Genesis 1:3*[1]

 TO SPEAK IS GOOD; to communicate is better; to be understood is best of all. Speech is a marvelous gift from God, and it is powerful, creative, and redemptive. No one understood this better than Martin Luther, as we see above. The Word, in and of itself a marvel, is good. Yet it carries with it a great power to bring something out of nothingness. Genesis 1:3 and John 1:1 are two of the greatest testimonies to this truth. God speaks "Light," and there is light. God speaks the words "Jesus Christ," and there is redemption. Language is power, and though power may not

reside in our words as it does in God's Word, there is power there, nonetheless, perhaps a reflection of God's image in us.

We sometimes speak as if words don't matter. The phrase one hears, "It's just rhetoric," points to a type of empty language where the word seems distant from the act. When words and actions don't come together, it is a disappointment. What makes it such a disappointment is that the very saying of a word, even now, carries the expectation (or at least the hope) that what the word signifies will become incarnate, will become real to us.

Words play a significant role in the grief process, and the whole point of trying to express grief is not only to hear the words but also to communicate the reality, to incarnate it in some way, so that it can be dealt with. This incarnation seems to come to fruition at the point of understanding. To speak grief, to communicate grief until it is incarnate, and then to see that grief, in word incarnate, taken into another person in sympathetic understanding, looks like a most religious act to me. In this way we can share one another's burdens, as St. Paul admonishes us in Galatians 6:2. If you ever want to read a novel that tries to embody this notion, try Charles Williams' *Descent into Hell*. There we see a man who convinces a woman to let him help her carry a burden. She is skeptical, at first unwilling, yet she finally allows him to help, and it does help.[2]

My family has been lucky. We have had the good fortune to have a counselor who understands the importance of expressing grief, of trying to speak out the reality that breaks our hearts, so that our hearts may be repaired. It's a simple principle, one that applies to physical repair as well as emotional and spiritual: You can't fix what's broken until you've located it. Words are the only maps we have to help navigate the area of the heart.

This is much harder than it sounds. How can we navigate the heart if the language of the heart has seeped out at the point of the break? This, as much as anything, speaks to why the bereaved seem to go into a shell after the death of a loved one. This explains why so little is said, so little expressed in the face of loss. The vessel that carries words for such an occasion is the very thing that has been damaged, and so repairs take a while.

I believe that in grief we are reduced to the status of children, and I want to explore that notion, in both its literal and metaphorical senses. I will do this by looking at my own children's experiences in counseling and how the move from silence to words transpires.

There are many stereotypes about children and grief, and one of the most common is that children do not grieve as deeply as adults. I remember reading an article where the author spoke of children's lack of emotional depth, which he believed explained why children do not grieve as deeply as adults. They simply are unable to, he said.

Having watched my children struggle with their grief, I believe their tolerance for grief may be less than an adult's. They have to grieve in shorter spurts in order to keep from being completely overwhelmed by their feelings of loss. The grief is as real and as deep, but it comes out a bit differently. The reason for that, I think, has to do with words and their power. Children, having learned in rudimentary form the language of the heart, must relearn it after a loss in order to speak into being, to incarnate, their feelings. This is a long process, especially for very young children. Because their tolerance for the intensity of grief is less, learning to speak grief's language may take them longer.

This results in something of an uncomfortable situation. Many folks think kids grieve in "kiddy" ways and therefore their grief is not to be taken as seriously as adult grief. The assumption is that kids "get over" things faster. In reality, in order to fully deal with the grief they have, children must spend a long period of time building up the emotional support and developing the emotional language necessary to begin to come to grips with death. I imagine a lot of

children's grief processes get short-circuited; the very thing
they need, lots of time, is what's assumed they don't need.
This may seem a wild generalization, yet it seems borne out
in my experience. Many people have raised their eyebrows
(literally or suggestively) when they learn that my children
have seen a counselor for a period of years now. The implied
question is always, "Shouldn't they be over it by now?" The
answer, from my point of view, is quite simple: No.

The incredible power — awful, scary power — that unspoken emotions have on children can only be broken by
weaving words around those emotions until they can be spoken and recognized, heard and understood. In case some
question the depth of these feelings, I have included some
pictures that my children have drawn; pictures that are a way
of expressing feelings they haven't mastered the words for
yet, but are working toward. They show the inside process-
ing that is going on in children coming to grips with ideas
that they don't have words for but are striving to express in
the language of art. In a patient setting, where the child is al-
lowed the time to build up a heart language appropriate for
his or her feelings, the words will come.

I've included two pictures by Gwynne and one by Mave.
Let's focus on Gwynne's first, after a little background
information.

Gwynne began seeing her counselor when she was five and
a half years old, about a year and a half after her mom's
death. She was old enough to start trying to talk about
things, and the counselor thought she was ready to begin to
come to grips with her mom's death, at least through play
and art.

About a year and a half into the process (at that point
she was verging on her seventh birthday), within a couple
of weeks, Gwynne produced two art pieces that were, essen-
tially, ways to pass the time at a restaurant. Both are drawn
on the back of paper placemats. Both were a way of expressing grief, but it was a grief so deep that it was still in the

language of art rather than words. Looking at the pictures, I think one gets an idea why it might take a long time to develop the words needed to express such emotions. My reaction to the first picture (see Figure 1 on the following page) was horror. Despair screamed out at me from the page, and I wondered how such a small child could survive such feelings. The picture is the saddest one I have ever seen, including pictures done by adults, in terms of communicating feelings of loss. Gwynne is in the foreground, the black lines under her eyes underscoring the eyes that have literally cried themselves out. It is not only the little girl in the picture who is sad; the whole world around her is sad. The sky is raining tears to match those on her face. To the left in the picture stand the three crosses. Jesus' crucifixion was on her mind. To the right, in the background, is a tombstone, with her mother's initials on it (M.D. for Melanie Davis, though Melanie used her maiden name, Lane. Gwynne doesn't always remember this). Jesus has died, her mom is dead, the picture person "Gwynne" despairs, and the world cries. How could I expect such a little girl to speak her despair, to say her grief, when the feelings she felt and expressed on the page left *me* speechless?

There are other feelings beside despair that grief evokes, and one of them is loneliness, isolation. It is true that I, Gwynne, Mave, and everyone else affected by Melanie's death should be thankful for those who remain. Thank God I do have Mave and Gwynne. But to say that does absolutely nothing to help one deal with the feelings of isolation and loneliness that come with the death of a loved one. Two living persons who remain do not make up for the one who has died. Human relationships are not a matter of mathematics. A great loss is isolating, no matter how many loved ones are around us. That is not because the ones who remain are somehow "inadequate" or "not good enough," though one sometimes hears this sentiment. It is because the loss, among other things, underscores the contingency and fragility of all

Figure 1

relationships. When a loved one dies, a bit of trust dies as well. One of the things that passes away with the deceased is certainty in the durability of relationships we count on. I think we feel alone in grief not because we are alone (if we are lucky enough to have family and friends remain) but because we fear the loss of other relationships. At least that may be part of it.

Gwynne's second picture (see Figure 2 on the following page) certainly captures the feeling of isolation and the way it is tied to grief, sadness, and loneliness. Off to the left are Mave and me, smiling and happy, obviously oblivious to Gwynne's situation. To the right is Gwynne, who is very sad. Hovering above her is Melanie in angel form, the way that Gwynne most often draws Melanie. There is a palpable connection between the two, as expressed in the way Gwynne has colored the space between the two of them. Angel Mommy is also sad.

When I asked Gwynne about the picture, she was able to talk about what was going on inside of her. She said that Mave and I didn't think about Mommy anymore and that she was the only one who thought about her. What's more, she said that she was the only one who was sad anymore, and Mommy was sad because Gwynne was sad. The sadness seemed to provide Gwynne a connection with her mom that was comforting (like my idea of grief as a warm jacket) but also isolating. She was sure Mave and I could not share her feelings. She had to have them alone. In her drawing and in her halting attempts to explain the picture, she echoed the words of Nicholas Wolterstorff, who, in *Lament for a Son*, speaks of how his grief over the death of his son worked to isolate him. His words bear repeating.

> I have been daily grateful for the friend who remarked that grief isolates. He did not only mean that I, grieving, am isolated from you, happy. He meant also that *shared* grief isolates the sharers from each other. Though united in that we are grieving, we grieve differently. As each death has its

Figure 2

own character, so too each grief over a death has its own character — its own inscape.[3]

Gwynne didn't have all the words of Wolterstorff; she did have some of the same feeling. As she continues in counseling, she will develop the language she will need to come to grips, time and time again in her life, with that which has broken her heart the most. I cannot journey with her through her "inscape," that which is inside and deepest in all of us, but her counselor and I both can give her support, can give her love, and can help her shape a language that will be useful as she makes her exploration.

This process can be seen at work in my oldest daughter's drawing. She started her counseling sessions before Melanie died, when she was six, and continued for almost three years. There came a time when she was "done." By this I don't mean that her grief was resolved but that she had developed some ways to express her grief that were good. Her counselor knew she had finished a stage when Mave had no more to say. Having expressed her grief in art, play, and finally words, she now had a language to express her grief and a comfort level necessary to do so. Because of her counseling, she knew that she could express her fears and sadness, her grief and, at times, despair, without those feelings destroying her emotionally. She felt safe giving voice to her grief.

In a checkup a little later with her counselor, Mave was able to say, "I can always talk to my dad" if she felt sad or her grief was working inside her. I took this to mean not that she was not able to talk to me before because I wouldn't listen, but that she now had the words and the power of those words to express herself. Of course, she will need other words later. As she matures, other questions, other feelings, other concerns appropriate to her age will emerge, and she will need to learn a fuller vocabulary of grief. But for now, she's gotten the ABCs of it down.

A picture by Mave (see Figure 3), drawn when she was almost eight, two years into counseling, shows her coming to grips with her situation. We're all a family in the picture, the three of us — me, Mave, Gwynne — together. And up above us is Mommy. It's clear the three of us are whole and happy, but that doesn't exclude Melanie. Mave simply recognizes that Melanie has moved above, but not beyond, us.

There's something to be learned here from the children's experiences. As an adult, I was bigger, stronger, smarter. I had more tools, emotionally and intellectually, to deal with grief — at least in theory. But when it came to experiencing such a devastating loss, I had no more *real* experience than my children. I, just like my children, had to find the words to express grief, experience their power, and use them in the process of healing.

The difference between myself and my children was not my greater experience. We all started at square one. In some ways, the biggest difference (all the worst for me) was my adult coping mechanism of deception. Because I had read about grief in school, because I had steeped myself in theological constructs surrounding issues of life and death, because I thought I knew the language of grief, I was able to deceive myself about how I was dealing with my own sorrow. Ever watchful and careful about the children in their grief, I turned an eye away from my own.

One of the biggest obstacles that stood in my way was the assumption I continued to share with many others that my faith, if it were true faith, should somehow allow me to short-circuit the full grief process. I kept looking for signs of resolution, pointers that I had "risen above" the feelings I had about Melanie's illness and death. I wrote a book on Melanie's illness and thought, "There! Finished!" I thought I could set my grief aside like a book manuscript. That way of thinking trapped me for a long period of time. Hoping to "resolve" my grief, I was actually hoping to avoid the frightening feelings that accompany grief. I was not nearly

Figure 3

as good at dealing with my grief as my children were with theirs. They did not have the intellectual tools to trick themselves into thinking they had been able to side step the very real issues of grief. I did.

An example is my own feelings of guilt, which have come up in this book again and again. Mave dealt with her guilty feelings in her dreams and later in her words as she spoke of things about which she felt guilty, such as the time she and Melanie had an argument at the swimming pool when she was five. My guilt, unexpressed and unacknowledged, ate away at my insides. Did I do enough? Could I have saved Melanie? What could I have done differently? I played that one over and over again in my mind. What *else* could I have done?

I even had myself (in my mind) killing Melanie. During the last few hours of her life, I gave the nurse permission to increase the morphine rate for Melanie. Of course the doctor had prescribed a range, and Melanie was at the low end of the range. The nurse said it would make Melanie more comfortable. Within a few hours, Melanie died. Of course, Melanie was dying; but did I kill her? Did the extra morphine slow her body's system so it couldn't rise to the occasion of the next breath, of the next heartbeat? My mind was tortured by these thoughts. During my most depressed state, I dwelt on it constantly, especially at night, feeling in the throes of death during those long hours. Referring back again to St. Augustine's description in the last chapter, my feelings reflected those of the damned: "not living, not dead, always dying." That was Melanie for me at night — always dying — and I with her.

On the third anniversary of Melanie's birthday after her death, these feelings sent me scurrying for a red marker. I wanted to draw the lines on my wrist where I would need to cut. I couldn't find a red marker. I kept thinking, "It's got to be red, it's got to be red, so everything will match." A rage for order in a moment of insane grief saved me. I talked to a counselor about my guilt-stricken conscience. The solution she provided was simple.

"Let yourself feel guilty," she advised. At first, I was a bit shocked. I expected her to assure me that, of course, I wasn't guilty. That clear knowledge of forensic innocence had nothing to do with my *feelings* of guilt. I had been trying to fight a heart fight with my head, and the counselor knew I didn't need a simple pronouncement of "not guilty." What I needed was to work through my feelings of guilt, no matter how irrational they might be (or better, nonrational). The only way I could do that was to actually allow myself to feel my feelings of guilt, to embrace them rather than suppress them. Her advice remains one of the best pieces of advice I have ever received. If not a lifesaver, it was close.

If God's Word is to have power, if light is to break over our souls, we must recognize the dark side and name it. Our unspoken dark words weave a shield that keeps out the light. How careless we Christians are not to recognize that the Bible's writers speak of darkness as well as light, and that it's the frank speaking of darkness that releases it so that light might shine inward. There is, of course, the entire Book of Job, but one of the most poetic and frank expressions of our dark thoughts comes from Jeremiah 15:18. Addressing God with *true* words, Jeremiah says, "Why is my pain unceasing, my wound incurable, refusing to be healed? Wilt thou be to me like a deceitful brook, like waters that fail?" This statement rings so much truer and deeper than Robert Frost's well-known yet disingenuous poem:

> I turned to speak to God
> About the world's despair;
> But to make matters worse
> I found God wasn't there.[4]

No one really turns to God with the existential anxiety that crushes the soul to speak of the "world's" despair. We turn to speak of our *own* despair, our own hurt, our own suffering. It is not God's absence that offends us; it is God's seeming failure. Waters that fail. The promise of quenched thirst run dry. This is the starting point; others are false.

If we are not honest about our hurt and pain, honest about the feeling of deception and betrayal, then our feelings will ball up inside us into an impenetrable sphere of darkness that spreads like a cancer. By denying our dark and doubting feelings and thoughts, we give free rein within our souls to those unnamed powers, and the ball grows. Without first being able to admit that he hated God, Martin Luther would never have been able to move to an affirmation of God's love. Luther felt God's hand on him like a death sentence, and he hated God for it.[5] Yet few in the Christian tradition can speak as tenderly of God's love as Luther, and his path to this understanding led through a dark forest of doubt and despair that had to be acknowledged.

In the same way, the children and I have been fortunate to have a guide through the paths of darkness. The gift given to us is the insight that, though the path of grief takes us through dark places, if we concentrate on moving along the path rather than being immobilized by the darkness, we are able to break out into the light. We have had words of good counsel from one who herself heeds and points to the Counselor. God accommodates to us, as God always does, in the manner in which we need it most. When God cries, "Let there be light!" there is, and God gives us help to find it.

Notes

1. Martin Luther, *Luther's Works*, vol. 1: *Lectures on Genesis, Chapters 1–5*, ed. Jaroslav Pelikan (St. Louis, Mo.: Concordia, 1958), 17.

2. Charles Williams, *Descent into Hell* (1937; repr., Grand Rapids, Mich.: Eerdmans, 1983).

3. Wolterstorff, *Lament for a Son*, 56.

4. Robert Frost, "Not All There," in *The Poetry of Robert Frost* (New York: Holt, Rinehart and Winston, 1969), 309.

5. On Luther's experience, see Roland H. Bainton, *Here I Stand: A Life of Martin Luther* (New York: New American Library, 1978), 29–45, esp. 44.

Chapter Eight

FAITH, LANGUAGE, AND THE RELIGIOUS IMAGINATION

Language [is] a vehicle for the unsayable.   — W. S. MERWIN[1]

Blessed are those who mourn, for they shall be comforted.

— JESUS[2]

She knew now that all acts of love are the measure of capacity for joy; its measure and its preparation, whether the joy comes or delays.   — CHARLES WILLIAMS, *Descent into Hell*[3]

Come, Thou Fount of every blessing, Tune my heart to sing Thy grace.   — ROBERT ROBINSON[4]

 THE SHOCK OF THE THOUGHT literally snapped my head. I was on a two-hour drive late at night. The weight of grief suffocated me. I was mulling events over in my mind — Melanie's illness, her death, the ensuing couple of years — and an image of Melanie in her Genevan gown, standing in the pulpit, flashed in my mind, followed by the words of Jesus, "Blessed are those who mourn." Another loose way to translate "blessed" is "happy." Happy are the mourners, Jesus was saying. The juxtaposition of my grief with the word *happy* sent rage through me, once the initial shock subsided. Over and over, mumbling to myself that late night, the lights of my van sending out pale beams into what seemed like utter darkness, road humming along, I asked —

I demanded — "What in the hell can that mean?" I meant the question literally. What in the *hell* could that mean, because in my despair I was in an existential hell. What, with the flames of hell having burned away happiness from my heart, could that sentence mean? Happy are the mourners. From that point on, I began a journey to try and understand if what Jesus said was true or if he was a liar. The choice was that stark for me.

In some ways, I was at an impasse. I could not reason my way around the words of Jesus. Mourners might be comforted, I thought, but when? How? I did not feel comfort. I awaited the magical transformation — grief-stricken the one minute, happy the next. I knew things would not work out that way, but I waited on Jesus to prove his words or to be shown a sham. From the time that head-snapping Scripture popped into my head until my mind loosened up enough to hear its message, I was on a two-month period of intense soul searching. Then, on one of my jaunts through the various works of C. S. Lewis, day began to dawn. In an essay in *Undeceptions*, Lewis talks about the Sermon on the Mount, from which the "Blessed are those who mourn" passage comes. In my own mind, I had often separated the Beatitudes from the kingdom ethics of Jesus, which read like demands. But for some reason, reading Lewis, it struck me that my plucking the Beatitudes from the rest of the sermon could not work. The effect would not be the same. I always thought of the Beatitudes as comfort, yet when I heard the words at the precise moment when they most applied to me — Happy are the mourners — they were no comfort. Lewis showed me why. This is what he says about the sermon:

> As to "caring for" the Sermon on the Mount, if "caring for" here means "liking" or "enjoying," I suppose no one "cares for" it. Who can *like* being knocked flat on his face by a sledge-hammer. I can hardly imagine a more deadly spiritual condition than that of a man who can read that passage with tranquil pleasure.[5]

After having read this passage, a few days later I came across this from Lewis's *Mere Christianity:*

> I quite agree that the Christian religion is, in the long run, a thing of unspeakable comfort. But it does not begin in comfort; it begins in the dismay that I have been describing, and it is no use at all trying to go on to that comfort without going through that dismay.[6]

Though written in quite different contexts with quite different concerns by Lewis, my need drove these two passages together. For the first time, I realized that I expected a type of saccharine sweetness from the Sermon on the Mount's "Blessed" passages instead of a head-snapping sledgehammer. The real reason for my attitude was simple: I wanted the comfort without the dismay. What these passages from Lewis helped me discover was that getting at the comfort of the Beatitudes requires a dismay literally capable of dismantling my own attitudes. God intended comfort, but real comfort could only come at the expense of giving up my own self-conceived notion of what comfort had to look like.

Happy are the mourners! The final piece of the puzzle snapped into place, of all places, in a television sitcom. I struggled to make sense of Jesus' words, relying heavily on C. S. Lewis's insights, looking for the "more" that had to be there, trying to incorporate the dismay with the comfort. Then I sat down to watch about ten minutes of a short-lived sitcom. On the "George Carlin Show," there sat Carlin, spinning out this bit of wisdom: The single largest contributor to unhappiness is the pursuit of happiness. It was a statement against the American cult of happiness — the "me first" attitude that resembles nothing so much as Luther's definition of sin, which is that sin has to do with being self-absorbed.[7] Here is where the American cult of happiness is deadly. It is an invitation to think that the satisfaction of the self, apart from the environment and world in which we find ourselves, can be possible. In other words, happiness has been so personalized and privatized that people seek happiness primarily within themselves.

What kind of happiness can that bring? Happiness pursued in that manner can never be fulfilling, because its fulfillment depends on nothing but our own narrow selves. "No man is an island," proclaimed John Donne.[8] A *New Yorker* cartoon once ran that caption under the picture of a single man on an island. The man was all mixed-up — head and arms and legs all in the wrong places. We as *humans* can not make much of ourselves if our "self" is all we have to work with. We inevitably end up with the parts in the wrong places, and then we wonder why we're not happy.

"Happy are the mourners!" Jesus said. It's not that happiness is wrong or that Jesus thought people should be unhappy. The point is that Jesus understood happiness differently from much of our self-absorbed pop culture, the one that glitzes instantaneous gratification across the cultural landscape, offering privatized havens of happiness. Jesus knew that is not happiness.

Jesus' Beatitudes are a call to the imagination to see, speak, and sing the world differently. Look at his words. "Happy are those who . . . " and then fill in the blank. How does he fill in the blank? With all kinds of bad things: poverty, misery, mourning, suffering. So what is Jesus talking about here? What is the promise of the Beatitudes, of the Happiness of the Kingdom of God? The Beatitudes represent a promise that God makes happy (not eliminates suffering) in the midst of *real* life. Real life sometimes includes a lot of not-so-great stuff. But look at how the promise is set up: Happiness is offered to those in the midst of life, full life, life engaged with other people, life experienced in the world all around. God doesn't make us happy despite suffering but in the midst of and through suffering. Happiness is not a vacuous state devoid of problems; it is an involvement with the world in its suffering and being able to join in the common human task of sharing that suffering.

Sound nonsensical? It may. It certainly sounds a lot harder — and a great deal more challenging — than what I want at times. The best example I have to begin to unravel this mystery — and God's happiness, just as God's love, is mysterious — is two separate accounts I have heard of Desmond Tutu, the Anglican archbishop of South Africa. Both of those accounts, told years and miles apart, emphasized the same thing: Bishop Tutu's laugh. Here was a man who had seen great suffering and suffered through apartheid with the peoples of South Africa. He had been witness to things probably unimaginable to most of us. He had given his life over to his flock and the good of his people, which had involved him in life at its darkest and grimiest. Both persons remarked on his extraordinary laugh, and both had the same explanation. It is real life and real suffering that make for real laughter, for happiness is not running from life but embracing it in all its chameleon-like moods.

The Apostle Paul speaks of being baptized into Christ; he also declares that we are to put on Christ.[9] If, as I suggested earlier, Jesus can be seen as the face of God's grief, then to put on Christ is to open ourselves to the grief of God. To put on Christ is to stand with Jesus overlooking our own personal Jerusalems, the cities of our hearts, and weeping over them.[10] To put on Christ is to put on the capacity of Christ to suffer with fellow human beings. To be baptized with Christ is not a one-minute conversion but a lifetime of coming to grips with the human situation and the way in which we take its grief upon ourselves. Joy (happiness) is only raised up within us to the extent that we are willing to be baptized into a world of suffering. Why? Because it is the person who loves and cares who suffers.

To participate in divine love, we must understand divine grief and loss. To participate in divine love is to participate in hurt and sorrow and grief and embrace them, not run and hide, hoping for a miraculous happiness that whisks away the dark night of the soul. Jesus' own dark night in the garden, sweating, came before crucifixion, but it was also a prelude to resurrection.[11] To throw oneself into hurt, as Jesus threw himself onto the cross, gives way to the tomb's stone finally being rolled away and the power of love striding forth.

Paul says that we participate in the body of Christ (1 Corinthians 10:16) — a body that was ravaged by the hurt of the world. There is the bridge, the beginning pathway, to a union with God. Opening ourselves to God's love is an opening of ourselves to the hurt God bears. Christ became human, the ancient church writers declared, that humans might become God.[12] The American cult of happiness, or any cult of happiness devoid of the heavenly imagination it takes to see the world differently than our own narrow eyesight allows, keeps us from seeing that the essential step in that process of becoming more and more Godlike, more and more Christlike, is the ability to see suffering and grief for what they are: an avenue of love.

Christianity is not proof against suffering but its embrace. The road to happiness, true happiness, is not a detour God provides for us around our griefs but a route along which God walks with us, coaching us, so that we might learn to walk along the paths of not only our own pain but of others as well. We can be, as Luther often admonished, Christs to one another[13] only to the extent that we are willing to give ourselves to others. Christianity does not make everything all right, at least not in the banal sense that if one is simply faithful enough all bad things go away or that bad things do not hurt us. No, Christianity is not that. Christianity is the Beatitudes, which teach that joy comes in the midst of pain, gladness in the middle of suffering, and recognition of the goodness of life flashes at the moment of deepest grief. Christianity is a living of life to its fullest, and life at its fullest includes life at its most grievous. Christianity, as Jesus' Beatitudes show, is a new way of seeing, a new way of hearing. The Beatitudes must, as Lewis understood, knock away the sight of our physical eyes with sledgehammer blows so that the spiritual eyes might be opened to how Jesus saw the world.

Happy are the mourners! Jesus promises comfort. Later, in the Book of Revelation, we are promised that all tears shall be wiped away (Revelation 7:17; 21:4). Only with the imagination of faith can one see that, yes, there will be a time of no more tears, but it is only through tears that we can get there — God's tears, our own tears, our children's, and all those with whom we suffer.

A number of writers have spoken of God's "terrible goodness" in one form or another. George MacDonald wrote, "What a good — a good so great that I need faith to give the courage to face it."[14] Charles Williams speaks of salvation as a "frightening good."[15] C. S. Lewis, in his Narnia stories, reminds readers that Aslan, the Christ figure, "isn't safe";[16] he is terrifying at times. In one of my favorite passages, Frederick Buechner intimates that there is "something more terrible than the face of death — the face of love."[17]

God's love is a wild love that throws itself into the human situation with abandon, and it is a love that conquers not through retreat from but by marching into the heart of the forces that assail all of us. The happiness, the joy that God promises, is related to God's own work. Indeed, as Williams reminds us at the beginning of the chapter, all acts of love are the measure of capacity for joy. God's joy is infinite because his love is infinite, and Jesus' cry from the cross — "My God, my God, why have you forsaken me?" — is the eternal trumpet blast that sounds God's ultimate act of love. There can only be joy in the work of the cross, because its work was God entering into our pain.

There is no common sense about any of this, and one of the severest restrictions on Christianity's force is when people try to claim for it a type of "common sense" mentality. Any one who can read the gospel story and say, "Well, of course, that makes sense," has missed the point of the gospel. The gospel is many things, but one thing it is not is a book of common-sense platitudes. There is nothing common sense about the Sermon on the Mount. It is only at the point at which our constructs of common sense break that something else can begin to happen: Our minds can be transformed to see a different reality, the Kingdom of God.

The fullest understanding of the gospel comes, I believe, when the element of the "baptized imagination" is appreciated.[18] As important as theology is, it is at best an organizing principle for insight that is most often a matter of the leap of truly transformed religious imagination. Ursula Le Guin, fantasy writer extraordinaire, once wrote that truth is a matter of the imagination.[19] Maybe that is why Jesus spoke so often in parables. Parables are nonliteral, full of metaphor, brimming with suggestion, and they rely more on flashes of intuition for their real impact than on the plodding unpacking to which they are usually subjected. Parables paint pictures that are not common sense and that rely on those pictures to pique the imagination so that a new way of seeing can emerge.

Robertson Davies, the late Canadian author whose remarkable imagination was a source of tremendous delight for me, once said of that quality, "The imagination is a cauldron, not a filing cabinet."[20] The Kingdom of God, its whole way of being for us, may be more akin to something that percolates inside us, something that bubbles to the surface, than to the orderly filing of doctrinal briefs. Why is this an important distinction? Because different ingredients can bump into one another in a boiling cauldron, the flavor of one thing seeping out and embracing another. It's the mix of a good stew that makes it good. In a filing cabinet, the whole point is to keep different things separate — *a* for apple and *z* for zebra, with twenty-four letters in between making sure that the two don't mix.

Happy are those who mourn! If, as W. S. Merwin says, "Language [is] a vehicle for the unsayable," then what's going on when we try to talk of death and the grief it spills out in the same breath as religious hope? It is the recognition that language is not the master but the helper of our most deeply felt affections. That which does sit most deeply within us — love, joy, sorrow, grief — are unsayable. We feel them, but words are inadequate. To impose language, to make it the master of these feelings, to use the gift of language to file away these feelings both misuses language and misunderstands its power. The "unsayable" is best seen in pictures, heard in sounds such as "The Lark Ascending," or grasped by the intuition of parable. Language gives rough shape to these things of the imagination without taming them. Language is the translator by which imagination is expressed but not contained. It is a pointer, not a destination. The proper expression of the imagination is always metaphoric and poetic, suggestive and intuitive, and the point of theology should be to clarify this imaginative work, not replace it. The point of the filing cabinet of reason should be to file the records of good stew making. Theology is the recipe card, and it serves not only a useful but also a very important function. But to confuse the recipe with the stew makes for poor eating.

The Christian imagination is important because it is a way to get at some of our deepest experiences when the language of common sense has failed. At the time of Melanie's death, there were no words that really conveyed the great burden I felt. My own death seemed a happy exit from this world of silence. The flip side is that great joy also has no words. At the boundaries of life — life at an end, where shadows fall, and life at its fullest, where light drives out all shadows — there is no language, just images and sounds and tastes that mix together. The psalmist proclaims, "O taste and see that the Lord is good" (Psalm 34:8). I hear "The Lark Ascending" in my imagination, I see the flight upward, and I feel a joy that breaks the bonds of human language.

In *The Silver Chair*, C. S. Lewis's protagonists are trapped underground and confronted by the queen of that underworld. She is on the verge of convincing them, by hypnotic and common-sense-sounding words, that the "overworld" is only imaginary; only the dark cavelike dwellings beneath are real. In one of the most powerful statements on the worth of imagination I have ever read, Lewis's down-in-the-mouth marshwiggle, a fellow named Puddleglum, replies:

> Suppose we *have* only dreamed, or made up, all those things — trees and grass and sun and moon and stars and Aslan himself. Suppose we have. Then all I can say is that, in that case, the made-up things seem a good deal more important than the real ones. Suppose this black pit of a kingdom of yours *is* the only world. Well, it strikes me as a pretty poor one. We're just babies making up a game, if you're right. But four babies playing a game can make a play-world which licks your real world hollow.[21]

The Sermon on the Mount sends out the clarion call to imagine a joy that licks the so-called real world hollow. It is a call to follow Puddleglum's intuition and imagine the ways God is present with us in our living. It is a call for God to come, to be our fount of blessing, and to tune our hearts to hear, to echo, then finally to sing the songs of grace. The leap of faith required for that is the leap of the imagination that sees with Kingdom eyes the overlay of goodness on sadness and views sorrow as an entering into love. The words of the Sermon on the Mount are, with ears tuned by Kingdom imagination, part of the music of grace when loss lives on.

Language can, if used properly, call out this imagination if its purpose is to call out rather than control; if its purpose is to create as the one Word creates, rather than simply use hollow earthly voice to describe the common-sense world. Perhaps one example will suffice to show what I mean.

"Friends: This is the joyful feast of the people of God! They shall come from east and west, and north and south, and sit together in the kingdom of God."[22] So reads the opening words (the most powerful opening words I know) for a Presbyterian service of communion. "Friends: This is the joyful feast of the people of God!" There is no feast, only a small piece of bread that gets broken and a sip of juice that barely wets the throat, and yet, in this eucharistic celebration (*Eucharist* literally means "to give thanks") there is a cause for thanksgiving. For if we let ourselves see the bread that is broken and if we taste the fruit of the vine, there is more there than the words. There is the whole drama of Christian life played out before us, if we have the imagination and the eyes of the Kingdom to see it. The same Jesus who says, "Happy are the mourners!" also proclaims, "This is my body, broken for you." What both have in common, and what the Kingdom eye can see and the Kingdom ear can hear if transformed by the power of the spirit of God, is that in brokenness there is wholeness; in sorrow, there is comfort; in death, there is life. What both proclaim, and what the Eucharist shows forth in its feast of love, is that in the mess of swirling events we call life and death, there is God. That is the gospel truth, and there is no other. The point of the sacrament is to, through its power to direct the eye of faith to things beyond the common sensical, point to the feast to which God calls us.

The words of my favorite hymn sing out, "Be thou my vision, O Lord of my heart. Nought be all else to me save that thou art."[23] The song is a call to see God in life and death. It is a call to see beyond what we see on our own, and it encourages us to hear a voice not limited by human language and to listen with the ear of faith for a witness to that vision.

At times I have been on the verge, at the edge of the abyss because of my lack of vision. Though the proverbial abyss may seem a cliché, clichés get started because they embody truth. If I seek God's vision, if I look at the face of Christ, then the eye of faith grows accustomed to the light of the Kingdom and sees that, in a time of loss, the point is not to avoid grief. The pain has not gone away five years after Melanie's death, nor will it ever in this lifetime. But the vision is that, with God's help, grief is put into a new context. As life moves along, as grace envelopes, as the vision brightens, as the music crescendos, the pain of grief doesn't diminish, but life grows larger. If in my life I can hear joy, if song can be sung, if laughter can shake, if friends can embrace, then I can rejoice, not despite my grief but through it. If I do not have the words to really explain it all, then I can at least point to the one Word, who not only speaks but fills hearts and minds with images of God's love.

Be thou my vision, O Lord of my heart.

Notes

1. W. S. Merwin, *Regions of Memory: Uncollected Prose, 1949–82*, ed. Ed Folson and Cary Nelson (Urbana: University of Illinois Press, 1987), 199.

2. Matthew 5:4.

3. Williams, *Descent into Hell*, 171.

4. Robert Robinson, "Come, Thou Fount of Every Blessing," 1758.

5. C. S. Lewis, *Undeceptions*, cited in *The Essential C. S. Lewis*, 347.

6. Lewis, cited in *The Essential C. S. Lewis*, 311.

7. See note 7 in chapter 5.

8. John Donne, "Devotions 17," in *John Donne: Selections from Divine Poems, Sermons, Devotions, and Prayer*, ed. John Booty (New York: Paulist Press, 1990), 271–72.

9. Galatians 3:27; Romans 13:14.

10. Jesus overlooking Jerusalem is a reference to Matthew 23:37 and Luke 13:34.

11. Matthew 26:36; Mark 14:32.

12. Athanasius, *Orations Against the Arians*, in *The Trinitarian Controversy*, ed. William G. Rusch (Philadelphia: Fortress Press, 1980), 102.

13. Martin Luther, "Freedom of a Christian," in *Luther's Works, Vol. 31: Career of the Reformer I*, ed. Harold J. Grimm (Philadelphia: Fortress Press, 1957), 368.

14. MacDonald, *An Expression of Character*, 272.

15. Williams, *Descent into Hell*, 56.

16. The complete quote is "Who said anything about safe?

Course [Aslan] isn't safe. But he's good." C. S. Lewis, *The Lion, the Witch, and the Wardrobe* (New York: Macmillan, 1950), 64.

17. Buechner, *The Magnificent Defeat*, 18.

18. A reference to a previously cited phrase from C. S. Lewis. See note 12 in chapter 5.

19. Ursula K. Le Guin, Introduction to *The Left Hand of Darkness* (New York: Ace Books, 1976), page 6 of the unnumbered introduction.

20. Robertson Davies, cited in Judith Skelton Grant, *Robertson Davies: Man of Myth* (New York: Viking, 1994), 585.

21. C. S. Lewis, *The Silver Chair* (New York: Macmillan, 1953), 155.

22. *The Worshipbook*, 34.

23. "Be Thou My Vision," ancient Irish, trans. Mary Byrne, 1927.

EPILOGUE

Tell all you know. That's the only way I know of to praise the Lord. —John Updike[1]

For doubt is the hammer that breaks the windows clouded with human fancies, and lets in the pure light.

—George MacDonald[2]

 I STATED AT THE OUTSET of this book that it was written within the context of faith. I thought that was important to say because so much of the book reveals the despair that grief brings on. I have been asked, why write about it? Why write about all the bad stuff? Why explore such horrible feelings? Why not just let God take care of everything and be happy? How can it help to write about this stuff? It makes you unhappy and it just shows you to be a bit of a fraud, religiously.

This last remark in particular is troublesome, for two reasons. First, I think it is terribly unfair to question a person's faith for honestly dealing with questions of doubt. Second, at times I buy completely into the mentality, so that I *do* feel like a religious fraud when I can't make faith a pick-me-up for what ails me, at least not without a good deal of delayed gratification involved (something most of us aren't very good at). Why do this? Why expose myself — and I do feel exposed by this book — and why show what others may see as the "warts" of faith, if not faith's complete failure?

One reason is what MacDonald says above: Doubt is a positive force when used that way. Despair brings doubt. That should be clear. But what should also be clear is that what doubt clears away needs to be cleared away — an easy self-reliance, a faith in my own ability to have a good enough faith. Throughout this process there has been a constant bashing of my faith, and by the time it got bashed enough, all I could rely upon was grace.

I think others need to know how grief lingers and debilitates, not just right after the death of a loved one but for a long time afterward. In my experience, and I'm sure in others' as well, there's a tendency to get rushed; people want you to move on. I hope this book says, "Don't rush me. Walk with me instead."

Updike's comments, which I heard on public radio, are a reminder that we do God no favor by hiding things that are really a part of who and what we are. Tell all you know. Perhaps expressing my doubts and troubles praises the Lord as much as when I speak confidently of faith. Perhaps more so, because the former better characterizes real Christian life. It is not until we recognize that that we are open to the grace to grapple with doubt. In one of Melanie's many memorable phrases in her sermons, she said, "Doubt is the ants in the pants of faith that keeps you moving." I think she's right.

As long as doubt remains unacknowledged, there's no way to deal with it. As long as all of the bad things that go on during illness and death and grief remain unnamed, they keep our joy a shallow joy, for joy of depth comes from the same depths as despair — the deepest parts of the human heart. We can close the door on the one, but at the same time we're closing the door on the other.

Naming the bad, or at least outlining the bad with enough words to see its form, is a lesson I have learned and have tried to pass down to my children. One way I tried to do this was by writing a story that embodies the importance of naming the bad. During her illness, Melanie wrote a number of "purple flower fairy stories." These were stories to give the children hope and consolation as the purple flower fairy helped a sick mom and her child through the rough times.

I later took the idea and turned it into a full-length manuscript, where the purple flower fairy is clearly a Christ figure
helping a young child deal with the illness and eventual death
of her mom. One of the chapters explains in fairy-tale terms
what the importance of this book is for me: naming what's
bad so that its power is broken. So here, in purple flower
fairy form, is the reason for this book.

Dragonbane

Layne sat silently at the breakfast table. She scooped up the
remaining slice of banana from her cereal bowl, held it five
or six inches above the bottom-of-the-bowl pool of milk, and
dropped it. The milk splashed up the sides and ran out onto
the table in a couple of places. She was sure this would get
Dad's attention, but it didn't.

"Well," Layne exclaimed, "isn't this just a fine day!"

"Hmmm," came Dad's reply.

"School was fun yesterday." No reply. Layne thought for
a minute. "The teacher has decided to make every Friday
Mars day. We find out something different about Mars every
Friday."

"Hmmm," Dad eloquently replied.

"It was pretty neat. We're working on this great big ball,
a paper maché Mars."

"Hmmm," came the noise from behind the book Dad was
reading, perched precariously low over his cereal bowl. The
book was in danger of being milk doused if any of Dad's
cereal and banana didn't quite make it to his mouth. This
was a distinct possibility, Layne decided. Dad was paying as
much attention to his cereal as he was to her.

"We have homework, you know," Layne continued. With
a gleam in her eye, she stated calmly, "Trips to Mars, you
know. That sort of thing."

"Hmmm," ran the typical response this morning.

"Of course," Layne doggedly continued in her effort to get Dad's attention, "I'll have to hitchhike down to Florida. That's where the secret space shuttle to Mars is taking off tomorrow. Think I can get there in time?"

"Hmmm?"

"Get there in time. Do you think I can get there in time?"

"Uh-huh." The book was so close to Dad's nose Layne decided that, if she wanted to be mean, she could reach over, slam the book closed, one hand on each cover, and smash Dad's nose. She thought that might be funny — for the second or two it would take him to get really mad. She decided on another course of action for getting his attention.

"DAD!" Layne demanded as she shot out of her chair and stood next to him, yelling right into his ear.

"What is it, Layne?" Dad asked irritably. "I'm trying to read."

"I've been trying to talk to you all morning and you're not listening. Besides," she wondered out loud, "what's so interesting about that book that you're completely ignoring *me* this morning?" She ended with a tone of what she wanted to sound like indignation. It didn't come out right. Even she would have to admit that it sounded more like whining.

"Oh, well," Dad stuttered, as he tried quickly to gather his thoughts. "It's a book about imaging. ('m-ah-jean' is how the word sounded to Layne.) I thought it might be something your mom would like."

"What's imaging?" Layne asked.

Dad thought for a minute. "Remember when you played soccer last spring? To help you play better, I told you to make a picture in your head of kicking the ball into the goal. Remember?"

Layne remembered. It all seemed to be quite a big fuss over nothing. Her dad made her stand there during practice, close her eyes, and imagine kicking the ball, hard, really hard, straight into the goal. Layne had tried her best. She imagined all the right things. She just didn't kick the ball quite so well. In fact, her dad gave up on the idea when, after about a five-minute session of painting a picture of the perfect goal in her head, she kicked at the ball, skimmed her foot along the top of it (she was concentrating *too* hard, she thought), and watched it roll lamely toward the goal, stopping about a foot in front of it.

"It didn't work," Layne said.

"Okay, it didn't work for you just then, though I think it would have if you had just concentrated a little harder," Dad said, a bit of judgment peppering his voice. It was obvious that he thought it was a really good idea. Layne thought not.

"Anyway," Dad continued, "I've been reading this book on how a sick person can use her imagination to focus on an image, a good and healing image, that will help fight off the disease. I was thinking your mom might try this. It wouldn't hurt, at any rate, and it might help her feel there's something she can do to help herself get better. She feels pretty helpless, you know, just lying in the hospital all day, having people come in and poke and prod her, telling her what to do. That's hard for your mom. She's always been an 'in control' type of person."

That was certainly true, Layne thought. Her mom, before she was sick, was the most together person she knew. She worked, and was good at it, ran the house, and kept up with all of them. Mom was the one who scheduled things so they got done, and she had a way of making sure that, whoever was responsible for something, the work got done. Layne also knew that she wasn't the only person who thought this. Dad was always telling Mom how good she was at juggling so many things at once. Her granny, and many of Mom's friends, had also commented about it. Mom was just that kind of person. If she wanted something done, it got done. Period.

Of course, that was before Mom got sick. Now she seemed so tired, so out of it. Layne knew that the medicines made Mom sick, and the cancer made Mom sick, and several times she had heard her mom say to Dad, "If there was just something I could do instead of lie here all day." It sounded as if Dad had come up with something that would make Mom feel more in control, like she was doing something.

"Tell me more," Layne said.

"The book says," Dad started explaining, "that you can use mental pictures, things you think of in your head, to help fight off diseases. So, you think of the disease, you know, like your mom has, in some sort of image." Layne noticed that Dad avoided using the word for Mom's sickness. He didn't like to say it, and she knew he didn't like to hear it. Said it upset Mom too much.

Dad continued. "Let's say the image is a stray cat you don't want around the house. Then you think of the things in your body that fight disease in an image that goes after the bad image. Say, in this case, Mom thinks of a dog that goes after a cat and chases it off. By focusing on those images, she sends messages to her body to help herself win the fight against her, hmmm, illness."

Layne thought about it. She decided Dad had chosen the wrong image to begin with. Mom loved cats, even stray ones. But she was sure Dad was right about the main point — Mom would like feeling there was something she could do to fight off the disease in her body. "I'll help Mom think of something good," Layne assured Dad.

"Thanks, Layne," her dad said. "You know as well as I do that Mom needs all the help she can get right now."

With that, Layne and Dad got up from the table, cleared away the dishes, and got ready for their trip to the hospital.

Layne rushed in to hug her mom. There she sat in bed, her bald head uncovered, doing some cross-stitch. Dad came in with a big grin and an even bigger "I love you." Almost right away, without even asking what all the doctors had had to say for the day, Dad started to explain the book he had read. Layne could tell that Mom liked the idea from the start. The problem was, what images? Layne had been right.

Mom didn't like the cat and dog image at all. Then, after a moment, her eyes lit up, looking down at her cross-stitch and then up to her husband and daughter.

"Look at what I'm doing," she said. There, on the piece of cloth, Layne saw that her mom had almost completed a set of roses. The red one and white one were done, and she had the pink one half finished. "Since my problem is in my blood and killing my blood cells, maybe I can think of all the different blood parts as roses." Mom paused a moment, and then said, "Yes, it would all make sense. The red rose can be my red blood cells, the white one can be my white blood cells, and the pink one can be my platelets." Mom leaned back in bed, closed her eyes, looked inward, and said, "Let the roses bloom." Just that one act, Layne could tell, had a calming affect on her mom.

After a couple of minutes, Mom opened her eyes. "Dad tells me you were going to try to think of something for me," she said to Layne. "Did you come up with anything?"

Layne hesitated. Her mom seemed to like the rose image so well — such a soothing image — that she wasn't sure her mom would like what she had thought up.

"Come on, I can tell you've thought of something," Mom coaxed.

"Okay," Layne said, setting her hesitation aside. As she started talking, she got more excited because she really liked the image.

"Remember that story you read me once about the little girl who wanted to be a knight and wanted to fight dragons? But nobody would let her, because she was a girl. And then it turned out that she was the only one who had the power to follow the dragon through time, a trick the dragon always used to get away. And she fought, and won. Remember?"

"Yes, I remember," her mom said, smiling. "I like that story."

"Me too," Layne replied. "I thought you could imagine yourself as a knight, and the disease in your blood could be the dragon, and you could fight it and *win!*" Layne shouted in triumph and drew an imaginary sword from her side, thrusting it forward as if she had just killed a dragon.

Again, Mom laid back in bed, her eyes closed, her brow wrinkled in concentration. Finally, she opened her eyes and grinned. "Yes, that's a good image. Thank you, Layne."

Layne grinned herself. She liked helping her mom and making her happy. It made for a good hospital visit. When she and Dad left, Layne looked back through the door. Mom had already closed her eyes, seeing in her imagination her fight against cancer.

Later that night, Layne heard a quick tapping at the window. She rolled over and looked out. There was the purple flower fairy flitting about, impatient as he frantically knocked at the window. Layne rolled out of bed, ran over to the window, and opened it.

"We have to go, quickly!" the purple flower fairy said. He handed a pair of blood-red wings to Layne.

"Wait a minute," Layne said, "I don't much like this color."

"There's no time to lose," the fairy said. "Your mom's in trouble and needs your help. Only these wings can get you where we have to go."

Layne hurriedly put the wings on and was out of the window. They flew like mad to the hospital, then stopped just outside of Mom's window.

"The rest of the trip won't be like going through space, so be prepared. It will seem different." The fairy took Layne's hand.

All of a sudden, everything disappeared. Layne and the purple flower fairy seemed to be flying through absolute darkness. Layne knew she could trust the fairy, but this seemed so odd. Just as she was about to ask what was up, a speck of light appeared ahead. Faster and faster they flew toward the light. It got bigger and bigger. Then, the two of them seemed to shoot out of a tunnel, and the world was bright all around them, full daylight, with a wild country laid out before them. Layne was about to comment on the beauty of the wilderness — primitive seeming, she thought — when all at once she noticed a big, black burned-out spot ahead, as if everything around had been scorched. That's where the fairy was leading her. With astonishment practically popping her eyeballs out, she saw the cause of the desolation: a blood-red dragon, spouting fire.

Layne cried out to the fairy. "Look! Look! He's after someone! See how he shoots out the flame. There's something there, just on the edge of the fire."

They flew closer. Layne saw a knight in armor. At every furnace blast of dragon's breath, the knight held up a shield that turned back the flame. In the knight's other hand was a sword, or half a sword. It was broken. The knight was on the defensive.

As they flew ever closer, the fairy said, "The shield is the only thing protecting the knight now. It's a magic shield or else the knight would have been roasted early in the fight."

"What kind of magic?" Layne asked.

"There's a magical emblem emblazoned on the shield. As long as the emblem lasts, it will turn back the hot dragon's breath. But the emblem is fading — it wasn't made to keep off fire this hot forever, just long enough to get the knight close to strike a blow to the dragon's soft spot, there on his underbelly. But the sword looks as if it fell with an ill blow, hitting the diamond-hard scales that cover most of the dragon. No man-made metal can cut through dragon scales. The knight needs help, or it will end badly, I'm afraid."

Layne looked down again at the noble knight, shield up. She was close enough now to make out the emblem on the shield — it was three roses! A red one, a white one, and a pink one. They were literally wilting under the fire, each breath scorching the paint. The white rose looked especially bad — turning brown from the fierce heat.

Layne looked into the knight's face. Just then, the knight

threw open the helmet's visor and looked skyward, with a look that cried for help. It was Mom's face! Mom was the knight!

The fairy deftly led Layne to a position behind her mom, behind the power of the magic shield. There they were safe — at least as long as the shield held.

"Well timed," Layne's mom cried. "I don't know how much longer I can hold out. Each breath saps the strength of the shield's magic. Each breath comes in a little hotter, and I will soon be too exhausted to hold the shield up. There can't be much of the roses left," she said, regret filling her voice.

"What can we do?" Layne asked the fairy. Urgency was on her face. She could tell her mom couldn't last more than a couple of minutes. Just then, flame seared toward them. Layne let out a yelp. She looked down at her arms. They were bright red, just as if she had been out on the beach all day with no sun screen. A couple more breaths like that and they would be french fried.

"What can we do? Help us," Layne cried to the fairy.

"I've already helped as much as I can," the fairy said. "I was the one who fashioned the shield. I brought you here to help. I can do only one more thing, and that is to give you advice. Then the battle is yours."

Layne looked at the fairy, mouth open. She had not counted on this. She thought the purple flower fairy could do anything he wanted. Maybe he didn't want to help.

"No, Layne," the fairy replied to her thought. "I have helped. But there are some things you have to do for your-self — and that your mom has to do for herself — or you will eventually lose who it is you are."

The fiery blast screamed out. Flames curved around the shield as its power buckled. The shield was no longer turning the flame back. Soon they would be engulfed.

"Layne, if you are to stand a chance here today, you must do what all dragon fighters have had to do. You must be able to name the dragon. That will give you power over him.

The only chance you have against any of the bad things in life comes when you have the courage to call a thing by its name. Layne, name the dragon!"

"What?" Layne questioned. But, as she turned to look for the purple flower fairy, he was gone. What did that mean, name the dragon? How was she supposed to know the name of the dragon? She remembered back to some of the stories she had read, of how heroes of long ago searched far and wide to discover a dragon's name, going on many dangerous quests so that, at the most dangerous time of all — face to face with a dragon — they would have power. But she didn't have time to go on a quest. A few more flames and she and her mom would be done for. She sat down, legs crossed, and tried to concentrate.

She thought about all the names she knew. Dragons were bad, so it probably had a bad-sounding name. But what? What word could be bad enough to describe the life-gobbling monster? What was it that was about to eat up her mom and herself? Layne closed her eyes. Naming the bad. That would be hard. Even back in the hospital, she knew how hard that was. They never called Mom's cancer by its name; too upsetting, Dad had said. Better left unsaid, he assured her. They always talked around Mom's illness, but they never named it. Almost like it was a bad word. Layne wondered if her mom ever named the sickness, even in her imaging exercises. Or was it just too scary a word for her to use? Then, everything rushed in on Layne. All of a sudden, she knew!

At that moment, she heard a loud cry from her mom. The last breath of the dragon had curled the edges of the shield. Mom dropped to her knees, exhausted by the battle, strength sapped by the heat. Her shield lowered.

With a yelp of delight, the dragon leapt forward. He came down with a thunderous thud one step from Mom. The stink was horrible. There was a gurgling sound that Layne knew was the closest such an evil creature could come to laughter. With a wild and triumphant gleam in his eyes, the dragon raised his front leg, swung it down toward Mom, and knocked the shield away. Then, with the same gurgling laughter, a hideous voice exclaimed, "Now meet thy doom!" The creature raised itself on its back legs and inhaled enough air to make it feel like the wind was pulling Layne toward the monster. His chest filled, and he held there for a moment, heating it up for the last fiery blast that would incinerate Layne and her mom.

At that exact moment, Layne leapt up. She jumped beside Mom, looked up at the dragon just as he was beginning to exhale, and cried out, "Leukemia!"

That very instant, the dragon froze, just as if he were completely encased in ice. Raised up on his back feet, the dragon's soft underbelly was exposed. As quickly as her scorched flesh could move, Mom jumped to her feet. She took her half-sword, with its ragged edge where it had been broken, and buried it up to the hilt in dragon flesh. There was a scream of pain, and the dragon, freed in its death throes from the spell of his true name, came tumbling forward. Layne grabbed Mom's hand and pulled her to the side. The dragon hit the ground hard enough to make it shake. The force of the impact forced the air out of its lungs, so that flames shot out and ran along the ground for fifty feet. With one last effort, the dragon turned its head around, to look back at his conquerors. From the gleam of pure evil in his eye, Layne knew that he meant to take them with him. He again took in breath, though not with a tenth of the force as before. But then the gleam turned glazy in his eye, and the fire that shone there went out. The dragon was dead.

Layne and Mom collapsed on the ground, bone-scorched dry. Layne realized how thirsty she was. She looked at Mom and knew she had to have water right away, or she wouldn't make it. She tried to get up, but fell again. Dizziness spun her around. But just as she was falling unconscious, she felt water on her lips. She looked up and saw the purple flower fairy. He smiled at her. "Well done, Layne. A brave and courageous deed." Then Layne fell into darkness. She would have been amazed to see, if she had been awake, how the purple flower fairy, though so small, picked up both her and Mom and flew them home. After tucking Layne in bed, the fairy leaned over and whispered in her ear, "Remember, Layne, remember. Always name the things that you fear the most. Then the fear will be less, and your power more." And with that, he gently kissed her on the forehead and flew off into the night.

Notes

1. Interview with John Updike broadcast on "Fresh Air," WHYY, Philadelphia, June 1996.
2. MacDonald, *An Expression of Character*, 154.